What to Say
When You Don't Know
What to Say

What to Say
When You Don't Know
What to Say

Alice Fleming

Charles Scribner's Sons | New York

Copyright © 1982 Alice Fleming

Library of Congress Cataloging in Publication Data
Fleming, Alice Mulcahey, date
What to say when you don't know what to say.
Includes index.
Summary: Advice for making conversation, speaking
effectively, and saying the appropriate things at such
times as when making introductions, refusing invitations,
and attending formal ceremonies.
1. Youth—Conduct of life.   [1. Oral communication.
2. Communication.   3. Interpersonal relations]   I. Title.
BJ1661.F43   395'.123   82–5782
ISBN 0–684–17626–2   AACR2

3 5 7 9 11 13 15 17 19   F/C   20 18 16 14 12 10 8 6 4 2

Printed in the United States of America

Contents

v

1 | Why You Feel Tense, Timid, and Tongue-Tied

HAVE you ever felt embarrassed because you didn't know what to say? If the answer is yes, you're not alone. About a hundred million other people, including Elizabeth Taylor, Joe DiMaggio, Carol Burnett, Henry Fonda, Jackie Onassis, Prince Charles, and—would you believe?—Bette Midler, have all felt the same way.

Yours may be the flat-out, no-nonsense brand of embarrassment. If so, you know from experience what it's like. Your heart pounds, your hands sweat, your face gets flushed, your stomach does flip-flops. You don't know what to say, but even if you did, you couldn't say it; the words would get strangled in your throat.

Not everyone falls apart that totally, but most people develop a few nervous symptoms when they have to go somewhere or do something they're not used to, or talk to someone—or worse, several people—they don't know. If the affliction sounds familiar, you'll be interested

1

to know that psychologists have a name for it: social anxiety.

A few years ago, a Stanford University psychologist drew up a list of the situations that can bring on an attack of social anxiety. The two surefire panic producers, he discovered, are walking into a room full of strangers, and standing up and making a speech. Slightly less threatening but still high on everyone's rather-not-do list are:

1. talking to members of the opposite sex
2. meeting new people
3. going to parties and dances
4. speaking out in a group
5. talking to people in positions of authority (such as teachers and employers)
6. being the center of attention
7. talking to people who are older, richer, smarter, better-looking, or superior in some other way
8. asking for help

If you've ever felt tense, timid, or tongue-tied in any of these situations—or if you've been so chicken that you've gone out of your way to avoid them—you don't need a psychologist to tell you what they are; you need some advice on how to deal with them.

Before you learn the hows, though, you ought to know the whys. Why do certain situations have the power to turn otherwise normal people into quivering nerds?

At the heart of it all, the experts maintain, is a fear

of being rejected. When we step out of our familiar worlds and venture into unfamiliar ones, we become more aware of ourselves as social objects, more conscious of how we look and act, more concerned about the kind of impression we're making. Lurking in the back of our minds is the alarming suspicion that it won't be a very good one. That's what causes the trouble.

If you want to overcome your social anxiety and learn to talk to people with ease, you've got to get rid of the suspicion that they're not going to like you. The best way to do that is to stop dwelling on the reasons why they shouldn't.

"Nobody's perfect," as Charlie Brown keeps reminding us, but it's amazing how many people think they should be. They measure their looks against those of their favorite TV stars, their brains or athletic ability against the kids who win Ivy League scholarships. When they fall short—as they inevitably do—they're quick to write themselves off as failures.

Then there are the people who—no matter how many other things they've got going for them—can always find one fault that makes the rest seem worthless. They live in the wrong neighborhood. They have to wear glasses. They don't have a steady date.

When perfection is your yardstick, it's easy to single out a minor problem and escalate it into a major catastrophe. It's also easy to get so obsessed with your defects that you overlook your strong points.

Can you believe that when Lauren Hutton was a

teenager, she was ashamed of being skinny? That Phoebe Snow hated her frizzy hair? That Dustin Hoffman was self-conscious about being short? That Robert Young brooded about his beanpole build?

Their woes seem laughable now, and although none of them thought so at the time, they weren't worth agonizing over then either. Your own flaws—real or imagined—will seem just as trivial a few years from now, so if you're smart, you'll stop putting yourself down for things that can't be changed. Most of them are accidental details that have nothing to do with the real you—unless you use them as excuses to keep it hidden.

Eleanor Roosevelt said, "No one can make you feel inferior without your consent." Stop giving your consent, and stop being the first to run yourself down. You're as good as anyone else, and in some areas, you're a little better.

Instead of harping on what's wrong with you, give your ego a boost by looking at what's right. Do your friends compliment you on being thoughtful, playing a good game of volleyball, having nice eyes or a pleasant smile? Don't pooh-pooh such praise. They're probably sincere and they're probably right.

Can you do one thing especially well—dance, cook, draw, play chess? Be proud of it. That doesn't mean you have to go around bragging and showing off every chance you get. (If you do, it's a sure sign of an inferiority complex.) It does mean that you have at least one, and probably many more, reasons to think well of yourself and to assume that other people will do the same.

Learning to think well of yourself is the first step in curing your social anxiety. If your insecurities are so acute that you fear your condition may be terminal, you can learn to fake a self-confident style. Far from turning you into a phony, it will help you develop the real thing.

After that, all you need are some conversational skills. They're not as hard to acquire as you might think. In fact, the process isn't much different from learning to drive a car. You have to be prepared to take a few risks and make a few mistakes, but once you master the basic techniques, all the rest is mileage.

2 | How to Cope with Calamities

ONLY an idiot would drive a car without first finding out where the brakes are and what to do in case of a stall. Things can go wrong when you're talking, too. You know that—that's what scares you. But you won't be so scared if you also know how to extricate yourself from calamities.

Back in the early days of radio, Will Rogers, one of America's most famous comedians, was in a broadcasting studio with a young man who was about to make his debut as an announcer. The young man was ashen-faced.

"What's the matter?" asked Rogers.

"I'm petrified," the young man replied weakly. "Suppose I make a mistake?"

Rogers smiled. "Go ahead and make one," he said. "It'll make folks think you're almost as human as they are."

Will Rogers was a good amateur psychologist. The

professionals have since done studies showing that, far from being scornful of other people's mistakes, the rest of us are sympathetic because we can identify with their embarrassment.

Former President Gerald Ford is a good example. He was forever bumping his head on airplane doors, stumbling on steps, and saying things like, "Whenever I can, I always watch the Detroit Tigers on radio." In spite of this—or possibly because of it—Ford was one of the most popular presidents the country has had in recent years.

The most consoling thing about mistakes is that everybody makes them. You're not the only one who's announced that you hate cats only to be informed that the person to whom you announced it has three of them. Or said, "Who's that silly-looking guy with the funny hat?" and been told, "That's my brother."

At a prewedding party honoring Prince Charles, one of his friends turned to the groom-to-be and congratulated him on his forthcoming marriage to Lady Jane. It was an embarrassing remark, not only because the Prince's fiancee was Lady Diana, but because Lady Jane happened to be one of his former girl friends.

There isn't much to be done about such gaffes except apologize. When you pull one, say something like, "That wasn't too cool, was it? I'm sorry." Or, "I seem to have a talent for saying the wrong thing. I hope you'll forgive me."

The real problem about mistakes isn't that *the rest*

of the world won't forgive and forget them, it's that *we won't*. For some reason, we all seem to have a built-in need to keep berating ourselves for our blunders, to go over them again and again, and to persist in reminding ourselves—and everyone else—how stupid we were.

Carrying on about your mistakes in public won't make them go away. If anything, it prolongs your embarrassment and puts you in danger of becoming a bore about it as well. But there's no harm in unburdening yourself in private. In fact, it's a good idea. Tell your story to a close friend, someone who can sympathize with your plight but who can also assure you that you're not a complete dodo. This will shore up your self-esteem and may even get you to the point where you can laugh the whole thing off. Don't be surprised, though, if you never completely reach that point. Many people still get red-faced at the thought of an embarrassing episode that happened years before.

Psychologist André Modigliani of Harvard University did an experiment in which he divided a group of ninety-two subjects into teams and asked each team to solve a series of anagrams within ten minutes. Half the members were given anagrams that were unsolvable, and, as was expected, they failed at the task. The psychologist then observed their reactions to their embarrassment at letting their fellow team members down.

Modigliani reported that only two of the subjects said frankly, "I guess I blew it." The rest used various forms of a tactic the psychologist calls facework to make their teammates think better of them. These included:

1. defensively changing the subject ("How much longer is this thing going to go on?")
2. introducing information to excuse their performance ("Fluorescent lights really affect my concentration.")
3. minimizing failure by derogating the task ("For my money, solving anagrams is pretty meaningless and boring.")
4. denying failure ("Nobody could solve those in ten minutes.")
5. introducing redeeming or self-enhancing information ("I'm usually much better at mathematical-type tasks.")
6. fishing for reassurance ("I really messed you guys up pretty bad, didn't I?")

You've probably used one or another of these types of facework when you've messed up in some way. It's a natural reaction. As you may have discovered, however, trying to cover your tracks or come up with an alibi can make you feel as uncomfortable as messing up did in the first place. It's easier to say flatly, "I guess I blew it. I'm sorry." If nothing else, it ends the matter right then and there.

Unfortunately, not all mistakes can be disposed of

that easily. If you inadvertently make an insulting remark about a person's race, religion, or ethnic background—or say anything else that's mean as well as thoughtless—a more elaborate apology is in order. In addition to saying you're sorry, say that you've learned a lesson. You'll never make a potentially offensive remark to anyone, anywhere, ever again. And don't just say it, *mean* it.

Blunders are bad, but their most visible side effect, blushes, are even worse. Words can frequently be covered up with more words, but blushes are impossible to hide. Worse yet, when you realize you're blushing, you start to blush even more.

If you're fair skinned—and particularly if you're a redhead—blushing is more of a problem. It's not that you blush more than other people, it's just that your blushes are more apparent.

The nineteenth-century British scientist, Charles Darwin, who is better known for his theory of evolution, made one of the first and most complete studies of blushing. Darwin noted, among other things, that blushes occur only on the face, neck, and ears; that man is the only animal that blushes; and that, with the exception of infants and the severely mentally retarded, every member of the human race does it. Blushing is a sign of embarrassment, and you have to be aware of yourself as a social being before you can be embarrassed.

The two things that are most likely to make people blush are feeling conspicuous and feeling incompetent.

You're apt to feel both when you make a mistake, forget a name, give a wrong answer, or ask a silly question. If it happens in the classroom, you can sweat it out and resolve to be better prepared the next time. Or you can try to come up with an intelligent question, answer, or comment later in the period. The latter will make you feel better because it will prove to the rest of the class and—even more important—to yourself that you're not such a ninny after all.

In social situations, the best way to cool your blushes is to draw attention away from yourself as quickly as possible. Ask a question like, "What did you think of the way the Yankees played last night?" or "Did you see the article on John Travolta in yesterday's paper?" Another diversionary tactic is to comment on something elsewhere in the room—an interesting picture, an unusual piece of furniture, someone wearing an attractive or unique outfit.

What you want to do is elicit a response from somebody else. Let him take over the talking for a while so you can recover your self-confidence and give your blushes time to disappear.

Some years ago, Barbara Walters was interviewing a guest on the "Today" show when he happened to mention Dr. Albert Schweitzer, the winner of a Nobel Prize for his work as a medical missionary in Africa.

"How old is Dr. Schweitzer now?" Walters asked pleasantly.

Her guest replied, "He's dead."

Barbara Walters felt like dying too, but of course she didn't. Instead, she said quickly, "I'm so embarrassed. How stupid of me. I should have remembered that Dr. Schweitzer died some time ago." Then, without belaboring the matter, she went on with the interview.

Walters was sure she would receive tons of mail from viewers crowing over her ineptitude, but there wasn't a single letter. Her conclusion was similar to the one Will Rogers had arrived at several decades earlier. "They'd probably blundered a few times themselves," says Walters, "and were relieved to know they weren't alone."

Everyone says the wrong thing occasionally—although thankfully not in front of a television audience of several million people. It's awful, no question about it, but it isn't the end of the world. As Barbara Walters demonstrated, even the most embarrassing situation can be salvaged with a simple apology: "I'm sorry." "Forgive me." "How stupid of me."

After that, let the matter drop. The chances are good that you'll be more upset by the incident and remember it longer than anyone else in the room.

3 | Don't Be Handicapped by Bad Speech Habits

IF you hope to hold your own as a conversationalist, you have to remember that how you say things is as important as what you say. Even your most brilliant remarks will fall flat if people can't understand you or are distracted by the way you talk.

If you have a speech impediment—a lisp or a stutter, for instance—see what can be done to correct it. Only people who are thoughtless or immature make fun of such handicaps, but there are plenty of both kinds around. More to the point, a speech impediment can make you horribly self-conscious, which will aggravate your problem and make it even harder to talk.

If you have trouble speaking distinctly for any reason, ask your parents about the possibility of seeking professional help. Your family doctor or the nearest medical center can refer you to a speech therapist or speech disorders clinic. You can also inquire at the library for books that list such services. If you can't find—or afford—professional treatment, ask your librarian to recommend some self-help books on speech.

There are a number of speech habits that aren't classed as defects but can be almost as much of a handicap when it comes to making a good impression or trying to get your ideas across. Here are some of the most common problems. See if you're prone to any of them.

Mumbling

The average mumbler doesn't realize he—or she—is mumbling. He thinks he's just talking naturally—and, unfortunately, he is. Many people find it quite natural to run their words together, slide over syllables, and translate expressions like "did you" and "going to" into "dija" and "gonna." If that's your idea of natural, make an effort to improve on nature.

Take the time to pronounce each of your words distinctly. No dropped g's, swallowed t's, or lazy b's and d's. To do this, you have to get over your reluctance to move your lips.

If you're not sure whether your lips are in good working order, a speech teacher recommends the following test: look in the mirror and say to yourself, "Hi, you good-looking, wonderful, lovable creature."

You should see a half-inch strip of darkness between your upper and lower teeth while you're saying it. If you don't, you're not moving your lips, and you're probably also talking through your nose.

Some speech coaches advise their students to limber up their lips by reading aloud for fifteen minutes a day with a one-inch cork between their teeth. This keeps the mouth open wide enough for every syllable to get out. You may not want to do this exercise on a daily basis, but try it a few times so you'll know how you should sound. Then pretend the cork is between your teeth whenever you talk.

If speaking distinctly strikes you as silly or affected, turn on your radio or TV and listen to some of the professional announcers. Do they sound silly—or simply pleasant to listen to and easy to understand?

Swallowing Your Words

When people are nervous about speaking, they tend to swallow their words—which makes it difficult, if not impossible, to understand what they're saying.

If you've ever talked to a word-swallower, you know how tired you get of straining to understand them or saying, "What?" or "Excuse me," all the time. Sometimes you give up and smile politely. More often you excuse yourself as soon as you can and go talk to somebody else.

If other people keep saying, "What?" or "Excuse me," to you or deserting you in mid-conversation, you're the word-swallower. The first step in breaking the habit is to train yourself to stand or sit straight. Keep your shoulders back, your head up, and your weight evenly distributed on both feet. Now relax your throat and jaws and breathe deeply, letting the breath come from your diaphragm just as you do when you blow up a balloon.

Your diaphragm, in case nobody's told you, is in the center of your torso just below your ribcage and a couple of inches above your navel. Put your hand on your midriff, and you'll feel it move up and down as you inhale and exhale.

When you're speaking properly, the breath that supplies your vocal cords will come from your diaphragm. Keep your hand in place, take a deep breath, and say a few words. Notice how much stronger your voice is?

Train yourself to talk like that all the time. It will keep you from sounding strangled and reedy and enable you to project your voice without straining your vocal cords.

A strong voice conveys assurance and makes people want to listen to you. By the same token, when you see that you have an attentive audience, you'll feel more assured about talking to them.

Eye Trouble

Your eyes are as crucial as your mouth in making you an effective speaker. Establishing eye contact lets people know that you're interested in them and feel they're important. It also enables you to get some idea of how they're responding to you. Their facial expressions will tell you whether they're interested, amused, angry, or bored, thus giving you some valuable clues about what to say next.

If you're not in the habit of looking people in the eye, it will make you uncomfortable at first. Start by doing it for only a few seconds at a time. You'll soon begin to feel more comfortable. As you do, increase the length of time you maintain eye contact. You'll be happy to discover that this is an easy habit to initiate and maintain. The reason: once you get over your preliminary discomfort, you'll see an instant improvement in the response you get from other people.

Speeding

Nervousness tends to make people talk faster. If you're already a fast talker and you get in a tense situation, you may end up sounding like a tape played on fast forward.

Learn to talk at a reasonable speed, and force yourself to go even slower if you're reading a paper or speaking before a group. What's a reasonable speed? It's not posted as it is on the highways, but experts consider 250 words a minute extremely fast and 100 words a minute extremely slow. The acceptable rate is anywhere from 120 to 160 words a minute. If you want to know what your rate is, read something aloud and time yourself with a stop watch or a clock with a minute hand.

Chances are you'll err on the side of speed rather than slowness. Most people do. If you do talk slowly, it may be because you're from the South, where everyone talks that way. Or you may simply have gotten into the habit of pausing too long between words and sentences. You can remedy this by reading aloud. When you see words and phrases that belong together, say them that way. Pause briefly at the end of sentences and somewhat longer at the end of paragraphs. Keep reading aloud until your own speech follows the same pattern, and keep timing yourself until your pace improves.

Reading aloud is also the best remedy for talking too fast. Pause and take a breath at the end of phrases and when you come to a comma, colon, or semicolon. Take a deeper breath between sentences and an even deeper one at the end of each paragraph. Train yourself to stay at this pace when you're talking. Be sure to inhale and exhale slowly when you stop for breath. This will keep you from picking up speed and, as a by-product, will also help calm your nerves.

Two-Dollar Words

Two of the main purposes of language are to entertain and to inform. You won't accomplish either one if you insist on using obscure words and convoluted phrases. On the contrary, half the people you talk to won't understand what you're saying.

A few years ago, the newly appointed U.S. Ambassador to Great Britain was presented to Queen Elizabeth II. When the Queen asked him if he was enjoying his London residence, the Ambassador replied that he was experiencing "some discomfiture as a result of a need for elements of refurbishing."

As an eavesdropper remarked later, "The man was either overwhelmed by the circumstance or he was losing his mind."

No matter how overwhelming the circumstances, try not to give the impression that you're losing your mind. Don't strain for high-sounding expressions and what President Harry S. Truman used to call "two-dollar words." There's nothing wrong with plain English. It's warmer, less pretentious, and it doesn't require translation.

This doesn't mean that you can't liven up your language by trying out new words now and again. Check the dictionary first to be sure you're using and pronouncing them correctly. If you're a reader, you've probably built up an extensive vocabulary, but since you've read, rather than heard, the words, you may not be saying them properly. Look them up so you won't risk a mistake.

Be adventurous about using new words, but don't go overboard in an effort to dazzle your friends with your brains and good breeding. Only someone as self-assured as William F. Buckley can carry off an act like that.

X-Rated Language

If you're talking to anyone but your closest friends, you may have to bleep out some of your favorite expressions. Curses and four-letter words are used much more freely today than they were in previous generations. Some have become so common that their original vulgar meanings have been almost forgotten. Older people remember them, however, and are apt to be taken aback if they hear you say things that used to be grounds for getting your mouth washed out with soap.

X-rated language can also be offensive to people who aren't so old. Certainly it should never be used to prove that you're grown-up, sophisticated, or tough. There are plenty of words in the dictionary that are just as effective and far more imaginative.

It's hard to clean up your own act when your friends continue to be coarse, but there is an important advantage: you can stop worrying about when to use everyday words and when to trot out your Sunday best. If all your words are G-rated, you won't get confused.

Twitches and Tics

Nervous mannerisms are a foolproof way to distract people from what you're saying. They're also an ad for the fact that you suffer from social anxiety. The most common nervous habits include playing with your hair, crossing your legs and swinging one foot, fussing with your clothes, fooling with your jewelry, biting or picking your nails. Perhaps you've devised a few others to add to the inventory.

If you tend to be twitchy, it helps to hold something in your hands. That's why a lot of people smoke cigarettes and pipes, and why, in the old days, ladies used to carry

fans and lace handkerchiefs, and gentlemen sported walking sticks. Smoking isn't advisable for reasons of health,
but if you're someplace where you can hold a pen or
pencil in your hands without looking unnatural, try it.
Otherwise, find a comfortable place for your hands—in
your lap if you're seated, at your sides if you're not—and
keep them there.

If you can't overcome your urge to fidget, follow
the advice a veteran actress gave Helen Hayes when she
was starting her career on the stage. "When you feel
nervous and want to tense something, curl your toes,
dearie. They're inside your shoes and nobody will see
what you're doing."

Nervous mannerisms (voice expert Dorothy Sarnoff
calls them speech tics) can also crop up in your speech.
Even people who should know better often fill in the
pauses between their words with unnecessary sounds—
"you know," "I mean," "er," "um," "well." Sarnoff once
monitored a television interview with the late Hubert H.
Humphrey and counted thirty-one "I b'lieves" in forty
minutes.

Try listening to yourself sometime. If you can get
someone to tape you in conversation, so much the better.
If you have a speech tic, you'll notice it and realize how
weird it makes you sound right away.

The sooner you become conscious of your tics and
twitches, the sooner you can get to work on eliminating
them. Basically, it's a matter of will power. Put your will
to work, and weed them out.

Put-Off Posture

While your mind and your mouth are struggling to say something pleasant, the rest of your body may be undermining their efforts by saying, "I really don't want to talk to you at all."

Body language—the unconscious messages people send to each other through their posture and gestures—can be a major barrier to successful communication. Here's what happens: If you're afraid that people won't like you, you feel wary of approaching them. You don't want to stand or sit too close, you turn your head or body to one side to avoid a direct confrontation, your face becomes a mask, your eyes hesitate to seek contact.

You won't be aware of the message your body is sending, but other people will. They'll see you as hostile or indifferent, and they'll immediately feel the same way about you.

Try to develop the type of posture that says "come closer" instead of "go away." Begin by coming closer yourself. Make it a rule never to stand too far away from anyone you're talking to. Three to six feet is the best distance. You can't make personal contact with anyone who's farther away than six feet. On the other hand, anything closer than three feet is too intimate; you'll both feel uncomfortable.

Face people when you talk to them; don't keep your head or body turned even slightly away. When they're talking, register some response. Smile or nod your head occasionally or say, "Yes," "I see," or "Sure," to show that you're listening and are interested in what's being said.

Personal Appearance

Your clothes and grooming also convey a non-verbal message. If you insist on dressing like a slob, people will take it as a sign that you don't think very much of yourself—and if you don't, why should they? Improving your appearance will help you make a better impression and bolster your self-confidence in the bargain.

Wear clothes that are clean and well-fitting, feel comfortable, and are appropriate for the occasion. Take special care with your grooming, too. Shower daily, be sure your hair is clean as well as combed, and your make-up—if you wear it—is carefully and sparingly applied.

While you're at it, don't neglect the most important accessory of all—the expression on your face. Everyone gravitates toward people who seem friendly and approachable, so don't get in the habit of scowling or looking sullen or sour. Look as if you're happy about who you are and where you are. There's more than a grain of truth in that song from the Broadway musical *Annie*: "You're Never Fully Dressed Without a Smile."

4 | Getting Your Act Together

P SYCHIATRIST Eric Berne wrote a book about personal relationships called *What Do You Say After You Say Hello?* Unfortunately, Berne didn't answer another equally important question: How do you get up the nerve to say hello in the first place?

It takes a certain amount of courage to strike up a conversation with someone you don't know or walk into a room full of people you've never met. Socially anxious types are often tempted to imitate writer Joyce Carol Oates, who showed up at a New York literary party, took one look at the sea of faces confronting her, and turned around and went home.

Other people handle the problem by not going to large parties in the first place and staying far away from anyone they don't know. If you've ever tried that, you must have wondered occasionally what you missed.

It's hard to say which is worse: torturing yourself

24

about the interesting people you might have met if you'd showed up at a social gathering, or showing up and not meeting anyone because you were too paralyzed by fear to make the effort. The best solution, obviously, is to go and have a good time. What isn't so obvious is that you don't have to be socially secure to do it.

Insecure people tend to think that anyone who doesn't bumble and stammer the way they do is automatically secure. This isn't true. Nobody feels completely at ease all the time; it's just that some people are better at concealing their insecurities than others.

A U.S. senator's wife, who's an old hand at meeting the public, confesses that before walking into a party or reception she frequently has to pause to give herself a shot in the ego. "Don't panic," she tells herself. "You're as interesting, attractive, and competent as anyone you're going to meet."

It seems to work. The senator's wife is one of the most charming women in Washington, and only her closest friends have any idea that she isn't totally sure of herself.

The eminent psychoanalyst Erich Fromm said, "The psychic task which a person can and must set for himself is not to feel secure but to be able to tolerate insecurity." Learn to look on insecurity as a fact of life. Then you can stop feeling guilty, embarrassed, or defeated by it and turn your attention to developing strategies to conceal it.

You must know people who are normally rather shy but who have no qualms about taking jobs—as salesclerks or waiters, for instance—that require them to talk to total strangers. Equally surprising, they perform them with a minimum of anxiety. Why? Because they're playing a role.

You may also have noticed that you feel more secure being the hostess, rather than a guest, at a party, or taking tickets at a school play or dance, instead of being one of the crowd. Again, it's because you've got a role to play. There are set things a hostess, ticket-taker, salesclerk, or waiter says and does. If you say and do the same things, you cut down on your chances of making a mistake.

Some people play roles of one kind or another without realizing it. When they feel insecure they instinctively revert to a pose. There are several favorites. One is the Clown with his endless array of jokes, imitations, and outrageous remarks. Then there are the Babblers, who march in, seize control of the conversation, and won't (or, more accurately, *can't*) let go—even when they're reduced to prattling about what kind of shampoo they use. Another character you may recognize is the Snob—the cool superior person who impresses people but simultaneously scares them away.

If you've ever tried any of these roles, or studied anyone else in the parts, you may have seen their drawbacks. Clowns have to worry about their reviews: will people like them or will they dismiss them as loudmouths or show-offs? Babblers have to put up with the strain of nonstop talking, and they never get to hear what anyone

else has to say, besides. Snobs are apt to intimidate the
very people they want as friends.

None of these roles is much better than your natural,
nervous-wreck self, but there's no need to stick with that
one either. It's easy to find a more suitable role—one that
will not only disguise your discomfort but can make you
a star in the bargain.

Whenever Eleanor Roosevelt felt nervous about en-
tering a room full of strangers, she used to pretend she
was a queen going in to receive her subjects. If you're not
the royal type, find a commoner to copy. Pick out someone you know who has an easy way with people. Imitate
that person's behavior in social situations. Say the sort of
things you can imagine him saying; use the same facial
expressions and gestures, the same body language and
tone of voice. Another, even better, person to act like is
yourself. Be the person you'd be if you weren't so insecure.
Behave the way you would if you knew that everyone
you met was going to like you.

A great many politicians and performers have public
personalities that are much more outgoing than their
private ones. Johnny Carson, who is remarkably glib and
relaxed when he's the TV Johnny Carson, is a dramatic-
ally different person offstage. He's so ill at ease with people that he rarely goes to parties, and when he does go,
he arrives late, leaves early, and has very little to say while
he's there. An old friend of Carson's says, "Socially, he
doesn't exist. The reason is that there are no television

cameras in living rooms. If human beings had little red lights in the middle of their foreheads, Carson would be the greatest conversationalist on earth."

Any number of actors and actresses have admitted that they went into their profession as a way of compensating for their inferiority feelings. "Acting is a wonderful release for shy and terrified people," says actress, author, and TV personality Chris Chase. "It helps you to get away from your pitiful, disgusting self."

Let's hope you don't rate yourself that low, but if you do, role-playing will keep the rest of the world from finding out. Moreover, since no one will be able to see the real you, you can stop worrying about making a bad impression. You're not being judged; the person you're playing is.

You'll have to steel yourself for your first crack at playing your new role. If you think you need a dress rehearsal, the next time you're in a public place—a checkout counter or cafeteria line, for instance—pick out someone with a friendly face and do one of the following:

1. Make a remark about the weather. (Isn't this a beautiful—or dreadful—day?)
2. Ask a question. (Can you tell me where the nearest drugstore is?)
3. Pay the person a compliment. (I've been admiring your sweater. It's very attractive.)

Whatever you decide to say, remember to speak clearly, look at the person you're talking to, and *smile.*

Talking to strangers is a low-risk activity. You don't know them, you'll never see them again, so it's no big deal if you get a negative response. Ninety-nine times out of a hundred, though, you'll get a positive one. If not, don't blame yourself. The person you spoke to might have been deaf, bad-tempered, non-English speaking—or even more insecure than you are.

After you've tried out your act on strangers, you'll be ready to take on the people who matter to you. Slip into your new role every time you find yourself in a situation that makes you feel insecure. The more you play it, the more familiar it will become.

It's an odd fact that many people who have never even heard of role-playing do it instinctively when they're with members of the opposite sex. Unfortunately, the roles they choose—the Flirt, the Big Deal, Lover Boy, Little Me—aren't very original. Worse yet, if they work (and one of the reasons they're so popular is that they often do), you can find yourself in a quandary. If you drop your guard, you run the risk of having the other person drop you. If you keep it up, you're being dishonest. This can lead to some complicated and not very comfortable relationships.

There's no harm in playing a role with members of the opposite sex. Just remember to follow these three rules:

1. Make it a role that goes with—and isn't a substitute for—your true personality.
2. Be sure it's a role you like yourself in, not one you've selected solely to please the other person.
3. Choose a role that will make you attractive to everyone, not just members of the opposite sex.

In discussing how he created the characters he portrayed on the stage, Sir Laurence Olivier said that he began by assuming their outward masks and mannerisms. When he acted the way a character would act, Olivier soon began to feel the way that character would feel.

The same thing happens in real life. Act calm and confident, and you'll gradually begin to feel that way. Keep it up, and one of these days you'll be wondering whatever became of the social cipher you used to be.

5 | How to Start a Conversation

THE average conversation starts off slowly and rather predictably, so there's no need to worry about being eloquent right away. Most people would be thrown for a loop if you were. The first few minutes of a conversation are purposely neutral. This gives people time to establish contact and decide what they think of each other, what mood they're in, and what they want to talk about.

If you've ever taken the time to study how conversations work, you've noticed that they begin with a series of ritual questions and answers. In China, they used to ask, "How is your stomach?" Elsewhere, the most common ritual question is, "How are you?" and the ritual answer is, "Fine"—even if you aren't.

Other ritual questions include, "How's everything?" "What's new?" "What have you been doing with yourself?" plus an infinite variety of queries about the weather.

Some people shy away from weather talk on the grounds that it's trite. Trite or not, the weather has an advantage over other subjects: it's something everyone's qualified to talk about. Moreover, a cheerful, though trite, exchange about the temperature is infinitely preferable to saying nothing at all.

Ritual questions and answers are the accepted way of starting a conversation with someone you've either just met or haven't seen for a while. They can also be used in the middle of conversations. When you run out of things to say on one subject, a ritual question can be the bridge to another.

There will be occasions when you find yourself with people you don't know. If there isn't a mutual friend around to introduce you, do it yourself. "Hello, I'm so-and-so," is one of the simplest and most cordial opening lines in the world.

Conversations tend to evolve from general health-and-weather type questions to more specific ones: "Do you live around here?" "Where do you go to school?"

With adults you might ask "What sort of work do you do?" Did you grow up in this part of the country?" "How long have you lived in this town?"

Another tack you can take is to pay the person a compliment ("I like your ring. Is that your birthstone?") or comment on some aspect of his appearance ("I see you're wearing running shoes; do you run?"). You can also talk about what's going on around you: "Are you enjoying this party?" "This is my favorite Beatle's song; what's yours?"

As you can see, each of these remarks ends with a question. That's essential. A good conversation has the same easy back and forth rhythm as a game of Frisbee. Questions are the way to get it started.

If your question draws a one or two word response, don't assume that the other person doesn't want to play. He may be shy, too. Or perhaps he doesn't have much to say in response to your question. Keep trying; it may take several tosses to get the game going.

If starting a conversation with one person is an ordeal, trying to talk to three or four can be agony. "You" questions ("How are you?" "What do you think of this weather?") won't work with a crowd. If you wait for everyone to answer, you'll look as if you're taking a poll. Use "anyone" questions instead ("Has anyone seen Woody Allen's new movie?" "Did anyone go to the church carnival?"). Someone will venture a reply, and the ice will be broken. In case no one does, be prepared to follow up your question with a comment of your own. That should get things going.

General conversation is all but impossible with more than six people. If you find yourself in a larger group, select two or three people and direct your comments to them. Large groups eventually split off into smaller ones anyway. In conversation, as in Frisbee, too many players spoil the game.

Some people despair of being good conversationalists because they don't have anything clever or earthshaking to say. That attitude is unrealistic.

During the 1920s and 1930s, a group of New York writers, including poet Dorothy Parker, playwright George S. Kauffman, and humorist Robert Benchley, used to meet regularly for lunch at the Algonquin Hotel. Their conversations became legendary. From all accounts, every sentence sparkled with wit, every remark was worthy of a place in *Bartlett's Familiar Quotations*.

If there were times when the members of the Algonquin Round Table had humdrum chats about the weather or the food or the latest news, nobody mentions them. But there probably were a few. People tend to remember, write about—and embellish—clever conversations, while the run-of-the-mill ones are quickly forgotten.

Nevertheless, there are far more run-of-the-mill conversations than there are memorable ones. Don't fret if your quotes aren't quotable and your opinions will never go down in history. Most people converse for the same reason they play Frisbee—to enjoy themselves and to pass the time.

The English author Thomas Carlyle used to visit regularly with one of his closest friends. The two men would greet each other cordially, then sit in silence for several hours. When their visit was over, they would gravely thank each other for the splendid conversation.

That isn't most people's idea of splendid conversation—or indeed of conversation at all—but it satisfied the participants, and that's all a good conversation has to do.

Another notion that's way off the mark is that conversation is a contest in which people keep score and somebody has to win. There are people who regard talking as a form of competition; they aren't happy unless they can hog the limelight, talk the loudest, and get the most attention. But that's not conversing, it's performing—which is quite a different matter. When it's played as it should be, conversation is a game in which nobody keeps score and everybody wins.

Just as Frisbee consists of equal parts of throwing and catching, good conversation is equally divided between talking and listening. If you regularly bemoan the fact that you never know what to say, you could solve a good part of your problem by learning to listen.

Don't say you *do* listen. That may be what you think you're doing when you're too frightened to open your mouth; but the chances are that you're not listening to anyone else, you're listening to yourself—your thumping heart, your shallow breathing, the little voice inside your head that keeps broadcasting negative bulletins: *I can't talk. I'm too scared. I don't have anything to say. I'll make a fool of myself.*

If you can learn to listen—*really* listen—to other people, you won't be able to hear those self-centered and self-defeating sounds.

You may be fortunate enough to know someone who really listens to you—a parent or grandparent, a favorite teacher, or a special friend. Someone who asks you questions and is genuinely interested in your answers, who enjoys what you say, no matter how prosaic it is. That someone makes you feel important, right? You feel that he—or she—is important too, and you're always glad to spend some time with him. That's how good listeners affect people.

Good listening, like good talking, is a skill that takes practice. You have to learn to focus on what other people are telling you. You can't be thinking about what you're going to say when they finish. If you're truly listening, you never have to worry about that. Your response will follow quite naturally from what they say.

You can encourage people to talk by asking them questions about themselves. As long as your questions aren't too personal (like, "How much did you pay for that dress?" or "Is it true that your parents are getting divorced?"), you needn't worry about offending.

There's an old saying, "A bore talks about himself, a gossip talks about others, and a marvelous conversationalist talks about you." To some extent, most of us would agree. We all think we're special in some way and are pleased and flattered when somebody notices.

Sometimes a person will hold forth at some length on a subject in which he's particularly knowledgeable or interested. Don't feel you have to sit there without a sound. Ask questions if you don't understand something or want to know more about a particular matter. Asking questions isn't a sign of ignorance. The universe is a vast place; people who are well-informed about a great many things can be uninformed about a great many others. More to the point, people are never offended when they know something and you don't. On the contrary, they're delighted to have a chance to show off their knowledge and grateful to you for providing it.

It may happen that you know a great deal about whatever the person you're with is discussing—perhaps more than he does. Don't be too quick to say so. Not only will it make him feel stupid, but you could miss a chance to learn something new.

An amateur cook once buttonholed the great French chef, Antoine Gilly, and spent twenty minutes telling him how she made omelets. Gilly, who had long since mastered the art of omelet-making, listened attentively. Later, a friend offered Gilly his sympathies for having to endure such a bore. "Not at all," said the chef. "She has a special way of folding her omelets. I've never used her technique, but it sounds much better than mine. I'm going to try it."

Not everyone you meet is going to be fascinating. There will be a few you don't particularly like, but that's no reason to tune them out. Their interests, opinions, and experiences will give you a glimpse into other worlds and offer you some new perspectives on your own.

If you're genuinely interested in other people, you won't find it hard to listen to them. If you aren't, get interested. You'll be more interesting as a result.

6 | How to Keep a Conversation Going

HALF the world is composed of people who have something to say and can't," said Robert Frost, "and the other half of people who have nothing to say and keep on saying it."

Frost was a good poet, but his view of human nature was much too pessimistic. There are quite a few people who have things to say and say them very well. The following suggestions will help you be among them.

What Can You Say?

You don't have to lead an exciting life to have something to say. The whole world is at your disposal if you'll take the time to read and to watch something on TV besides the soaps and sitcoms.

Even if you couldn't care less about national and international affairs or what happens in the Superbowl, the World Series, or the Kentucky Derby, learn a few of the basic facts so you can ask an intelligent question if somebody else brings them up.

One way to keep in touch with what's going on in the world is to read the daily paper. You can't digest everything in it, but pick out one or two stories and follow those. Read the editorial pages and the columns from time to time as well. They'll sum up most of the current issues and provide you with the information you need to form your own opinions.

Newspapers also feature human interest stories, travel articles, and news of the entertainment world, which you'll find helpful in starting your own conversations or picking up on other people's.

Take a break from music occasionally and flip your radio dial to the stations that carry interviews, commentaries, and special reports. On TV, "Sixty Minutes" is always provocative and is usually an instantaneous talking point, especially with adults, because so many people watch it. The talk shows, the specials, and the interviews on "Today" and "Good Morning America" are good, too.

Dipping into a few magazines will give you an even wider range of topics to talk about. In addition to their coverage of national and world events, *Time* and *Newsweek* run some fascinating articles about medicine, art, books, business, and human behavior. Surely one of these topics will spark your interest. If not, there are several dozen other magazines, covering everything from cars to cooking, to choose from. Books—especially history, biography, and memoirs—will also broaden your horizons and provide you with conversational goodies.

When you're going to a party or dance or anywhere else where you'll have to converse, come prepared with two or three topics to talk about. You may not have to use them, but they'll be insurance against painful silences.

If you have a special interest—fashion, photography, sailing, or football—read up on it. Know something about its history and the people who became famous at it. You'll enjoy learning these things, and they'll enable you to discuss your specialty with authority as well as enthusiasm.

When you do hold forth on your hobby, try to gear your remarks to those who aren't as familiar with the terminology as you are. It is equally important—unless the entire room is hanging on your every syllable—to avoid delivering monologues. Pause occasionally, and give your listeners a chance to change the subject. Better still, change it yourself by directing a question to someone else.

No matter how much you know about a particular field, offer your information and opinions in a way that will draw others into a discussion. For example: "I saw a TV show the other night about mountain climbing; do you know anything about it?" or "I recently read an article about Milos Forman. Have you seen any of his movies?"

You'll enjoy talking more—and people will be more inclined to listen to you—if you refuse to take the position that any subject is better than silence. Don't fall into a half-hearted discussion about something you don't know, or care, much about. Try to steer the conversation toward subjects that appeal to you. If you're enthusiastic about what you have to say, other people will be, too.

Former New York Giants football star Roosevelt Grier was never much of a talker. He got in the habit of keeping his mouth shut as a child when he moved from Georgia to New Jersey and his northern playmates made fun of his southern accent. During the 1960s Grier met Senator Robert F. Kennedy and became a whole-hearted supporter of his civil rights programs. After Kennedy was assassinated in 1968, the football star found his voice. He began making public appearances, talking to people all over the country, urging them to continue fighting for Kennedy's goals.

You don't have to be imbued with the kind of political fervor that loosened Rosey Grier's tongue, but his story proves that when you get turned on by something your eagerness to share your enthusiasm squelches your worries about what to say.

What Not to Say

One of the primary rules of etiquette used to be that politics and religion were never discussed on social occasions. Nowadays, both subjects are discussed quite freely, and they make for some animated conversations. Nevertheless, they should be approached with caution.

Don't state your opinions in a way that implies that

anyone who doesn't share them is either a villain or a fool. There's a wide spectrum of opinion among responsible people on such subjects as abortion, marijuana, nuclear power, and capital punishment.

Be willing to listen to other people's points of view. You don't have to agree with them, but don't sneer or scoff at their opinions. Learn to disagree without being disagreeable. "I'm afraid I feel a little differently about that . . ." is a better lead-off for a rebuttal than, "You idiot! Can't you see how ridiculous that is?"

If you feel so strongly about an issue that you can't trust yourself to be civil to anyone who disagrees, keep your conversational cool by changing the subject. One way to do it is to say frankly, "I get so worked up about the E.R.A. that I can't really be very objective about it. Why don't we talk about something else? Do you have a favorite sport?"

Here are a few other don'ts to keep in mind if you want to be a more agreeable conversationalist:

1. Don't talk about illnesses or operations, especially at the dinner table. They make too many people squeamish.
2. Don't recite the plots of books, movies, plays, or TV shows. They take too long and are too hard to follow. If necessary, sum up the story—"It's a mystery set in London about a pair of jewel thieves"—and let it go at that.
3. Don't spread rumors or repeat vicious gossip. It's

mean and petty and makes you look bad besides.

4. Don't be too critical. Building up your own ego by tearing down your friends is a dead giveaway that you're insecure or jealous—or both.

5. Don't spend too much time talking about yourself. Your experiences and opinions will give a personal touch to any conversation, but an "I" in every sentence is the trademark of a bore.

6. Don't unload your personal problems on people you barely know. Your parents' disputes, your dreadful marks, or your sister's drug habit are not topics for public discussion. It may make you feel better to get them off your chest, but it will disturb everyone else—except the gossip mongers who'll be gathering tidbits for their next conversation. It's healthy to talk about your troubles, but do it with someone you're close to, someone who'll be sympathetic, supportive, and may also have some suggestions on how to help.

Stories and Jokes

Most people like to laugh, so unless it's a terribly somber occasion or you're with a notorious sourpuss, don't be afraid to inject some humor into the conversation. If you're with people you don't know very well, however, don't come on too strong. Go easy until you can find out whether they're in the mood to laugh and if they share your views of what's funny.

Off-color, racial, and ethnic jokes are always in bad taste. In fact, telling jokes at all is a risky business. You have to be careful to get in the right details and not to give away, or scramble, the punchlines. You also have to be sure you're telling a new joke, not some old chestnut that everybody's heard a million times.

If someone you're with tells a joke, try to laugh— even if it's not very funny—and don't say you heard it before—even if you did. Be careful, too, about following up somebody else's joke with one of your own. It can look as if you're trying to outdo him. Worse yet, it can trigger a round of joke-telling that will bring the conversation to a dead stop and produce few good laughs besides.

Generally speaking, stories about things that really happened are far superior to jokes, but telling them well is something of an art.

There's a story told around Dublin that when novelist James Joyce published his highly acclaimed *Ulysses*— which uses an unusual literary technique and is incredibly difficult to follow—his father shook his head sadly. "Poor Jimmy," sighed the elder Joyce, who was known in the local pubs as a great raconteur. "He never did know how to tell a good story."

You may not see yourself as a good storyteller—and if you aren't, don't strain to be. But if you have an eye for odd characters, unusual happenings, and amusing remarks, by all means make the most of it. Some people can weave marvelous tales around experiences that somebody else would find quite ordinary.

If nothing very interesting ever happens to you, you can find plenty of story material in newspaper and magazine articles or on radio and television interviews, not to mention in books. Biographies and autobiographies of people in the public eye—presidents, ambassadors, senators, movie directors, actors, writers, and tycoons—are good. So are books about a particular time and place— Paris in the 1920s or Hollywood in the 1930s.

There are several rules that anyone who wants to be a good storyteller should follow:

1. Don't launch into a story if you're going to draw a blank before you get to the end. Know where you're going and how you're going to get there before you begin.
2. Don't give your story a hype by announcing in advance, "This is a really hilarious story." Let your audience decide that for themselves.
3. Don't go to a party armed with a story and insist on telling it no matter what. Wait and see how the conversation develops. Tell your story if you can make it relevant to the topic at hand, or use it to change the subject when there's a lull. If it doesn't fit in, save it for another occasion.
4. Get your stories off to a fast start without going

into any long-winded explanations about where you heard them, or apologizing in advance for not telling them as well as you should.

5. Don't get bogged down by minor details. You'll lose your audience's attention instantly if you start out saying, "I heard a story about a man in Chicago, or was it Detroit? Oh wait, come to think of it, it was Boston. . . ." If it really doesn't matter, pick one or the other and get on with your story.

Abraham Lincoln owed much of his success as a politician to his gift for telling stories. He got most of them from a famous old joke book, *Joe Miller's Jests.* Then he personalized them by setting them in a nearby town and turning the main characters into farmers, lawyers, or preachers, as the occasion demanded.

Like most storytellers, Lincoln worked hard to develop his fund of good stories and to become an expert at telling them. If you hope to be a good storyteller, you'll have to work at it, too. Start by keeping an eye out for lively anecdotes. When you come across one, copy it into a notebook. Eventually you'll accumulate an impressive collection of stories, and you won't have to rack your brain to think of one.

Whether you write your stories down or not, give them some thought before telling them. Get the events in the proper sequence and have a few key phrases at hand so you won't have to grope for words. It will make you feel more confident if you go over your stories in private before telling them in public. You might even do it in front of a mirror so you can check your gestures and facial expressions to be sure you're getting the right effect.

When All Else Fails

It never hurts to have a few tricks up your sleeve for those occasions when no amount of questions, compliments, or bright remarks can get the conversation off the ground.

One old standby is, "What three things would you most like to have with you if you were stranded on a desert island?"

Debrett's Etiquette and Modern Manners—the British *Amy Vanderbilt*—suggests, "What's the nicest thing that happened to you today?"

Barbara Walters' favorite is, "If you were hospitalized for three months, but not really too sick, whom— and it can't be a relative—would you want in the next bed?"

Start a collection of similar questions in case you ever get stuck with someone whose vocal cords seem to be paralyzed. Some possibilities:

If you won a million dollars in a lottery, what would you do with it?

If you could visit any city in the world, which one would you choose?

If you could change places with any famous person, living or dead, who would it be?

Admittedly, there is an artificial quality to these kinds of questions, but artificiality is a small price to pay to bring a conversation back from the dead.

7 | Taking the Dread out of Dating

DEALING with members of the opposite sex—especially the ones to whom they feel attracted— throws most people off balance. Very together girls have been known to come apart when they get anywhere near a boy they like. Studies show that boys get even more unstrung—although that may be because they're under more pressure. No matter how far we've come along the road to equal rights, men usually make the first move when it comes to asking for dates . . . which means that they also run the greater risk of being turned down.

The fear of being turned down, of course, is what those tremors of anxiety are all about. Suppose the guy you've been admiring from afar doesn't go for girls who wear braces? Or the girl you've been thinking of asking for a date wouldn't be seen dead with a scrawny runt like you?

Even if these supposes turn out to be false, there's the next round to worry about. Suppose you get as far as the first date, and it turns out to be a disaster? Or the first one is okay, but the second one isn't?

The list of supposes goes on and on, but if you're dying—and at the same time, scared to death—to launch a romance with some special boy or girl, don't let your imagination race too far ahead. Keep your wits about you, take things one step at a time, and be aware that there's a limit to how much control you have over the situation. A lot depends on the other person and a lot more depends on fate.

The first step in any relationship is getting acquainted. In the Victorian era, a lady could start a conversation by dropping her glove and letting the gentleman in whom she was interested pick it up. These days, women don't always wear gloves, and when they drop them, they're likely to pick them up themselves.

The easiest way to start a conversation with someone you'd like to meet—or get to know better—is to ask a question: "How do you like the new math teacher?" "Do you know what time the library closes?" "That's a good-looking watch; does it tell the date, too?"

This may lead to a longer chat. If it doesn't, you've at least set the stage for another conversation the next time you see each other.

When you do meet again, try to make some refer-ence to your previous encounter: "I see you're still wearing that good-looking watch," or "Remember that day I was going to the library? They've changed the hours, and I made it with only five minutes to spare."

Keep your tone friendly but casual. Unless you're naturally vivacious, don't knock yourself out to be Mr. or Ms. Personality. Overdoing on the charm can scare some people off and make others think you're not for real.

If you haven't had much practice talking to members of the opposite sex, give yourself a warm-up with people who don't interest you romantically before taking on those who do. Look for opportunities to talk to boys and girls you meet in the course of your everyday activities. Say, "How's everything?" to the boy who works in the magazine store or the girl who sits next to you in Spanish. Start a conversation with a neighbor or with your friends' brothers or sisters. Encounters of this sort will build up your confidence and make it easier for you to find your voice when you want to talk to someone you like.

At the bottom of all these get-acquainted gestures is the unspoken hope that once you know each other, you'll want to know each other better. That means a date. If the boy you have your eye on doesn't ask for one, you may have—or be able to create—an opportunity to invite him. To a friend's party, for instance, or to come along on a group activity like skating or swimming, or to attend a concert or show for which you just happen to have an extra ticket.

Whoever makes the first move, asking for a date requires some advance planning. If you have the nerve—

and the chance—you may decide on a face-to-face invitation. Be forewarned, though; this can be ticklish. It's harder for the other person to say no, but it will also be harder for you to conceal your disappointment if he or she does.

Most people prefer to ask for a date by phone. It's a little more impersonal, you can choose a time when you feel up for the call, and you don't have to worry about body language or nervous mannerisms. Before you dial, think about what you're going to say.

If she—or he—isn't home, you may be tempted to hang up without leaving your name. Don't give in to the temptation. Leave both names, last as well as first, and while you're at it, ask what's a good time to call back. If your second call is expected, both you and the person you're calling will be better prepared for it.

When you reach your would-be date, introduce yourself, again giving your full name to be sure there's no mixup. Unless you're absolutely certain she'll remember you, remind her of how you know each other. ("Kevin Stack introduced us at the basketball game last week.")

She'll probably ask a ritual question like, "How are you?" or "What have you been doing with yourself?" If she doesn't, you should ask one, and then get directly to the purpose of your call. There's no point in prolonging your tension. Besides, she may be in the middle of dinner, homework, or an engrossing TV show.

With first dates, it's a good idea to have a specific plan: "I was wondering if you'd like to go to a movie on

Friday night." If the answer is yes, tell her what movie you have in mind and what time you'll pick her up. If you're going with a crowd, or another couple, or just the two of you, tell her that, too. Everyone likes to know what to expect on a date, and parents often want full details as well.

In these days of rapid communications, with letter-writing a dying art, extending an invitation by mail may seem ridiculously quaint. Most boys will dismiss it out of hand, but a girl who feels apprehensive about inviting a boy to a special party or dance may find it a lifesaver.

If the idea appeals to you, use good stationery, write legibly, and be sure you have the correct address. Make your note brief but include all the pertinent details. Here's a sample to give you the general idea:

Dear Michael,

My friend Jill Bradley is having a Sweet Sixteen party on Saturday, June 3, at eight o'clock. I'm hoping you'll come as my date.

The party will be dressier than usual—good clothes instead of T-shirts and jeans. I know it will be a lot of fun.

Please call me (873-6168) and let me know if you can come.

Sincerely,

Relying on the U.S. Postal Service will eliminate the fluttery feelings a phone call would entail. On the minus side, it will take longer to get an answer. You can be worried for days, wondering if he got your note, when he'll call, and what he'll say when he does.

Every invitation has the potential for being turned down. If the person you've asked says no, don't assume it's because he or she doesn't like you. She may honestly be doing something else that day. Ask if you can see her some other time. If she's interested, she'll be quick to say, "Sure." You can make another date right then and there if you'd like, or you can tell her you'll call again in a few days.

If her "sure" isn't that enthusiastic or if she turns you down when you do call back, there's reason to suspect that she isn't interested in you. If you're determined enough, you'll give it one more try. If it's still no go, set your sights on someone else.

When you're the one who's turning down a date, do it as considerately as possible. Be sure to say, "I'm sorry," and sound as if you mean it. Explain that you're busy on that particular day, but say, "Thank you for thinking of me." If you're telling a social lie—which is the kindest way of refusing invitations that don't appeal to you—there's no need to say anything more. You can go on being busy—and sorry—indefinitely, and sooner or later he'll get the message and stop calling.

If you honestly are both busy and sorry, you can

avoid any misunderstandings by offering a brief explanation of what you're doing: "It's my mother's birthday, and my father is taking us all out to dinner. Perhaps we can get together some other time."

He may not be prepared to make another date just then, but you've let him know you're not averse to the idea, so he needn't hesitate to call when he is.

If you pick up a girl at her home, one or both of her parents will probably be on hand. You may have the feeling that they're looking you over—and you're right. Don't take it amiss. Be glad they care enough about their daughter to want to meet her dates.

Shake hands with the adults and say, "Hi, how are you?" to any brothers and sisters who may be lurking about. Your conversation will probably be confined to ritual questions and answers, with the parents taking the lead. Don't count on it, however. Some adults are as ill at ease with young people as young people are with adults.

If you have to carry the conversational ball, you can say something about your plans for the evening. If you're going to a dance, you can talk about where it's being held and who's providing the music. If it's a movie, mention who's in it, what it's about, or what the reviewers thought of it. (If you don't know, try to find out. It will be a good topic of conversation with your date, too.)

You can compliment a girl's parents on their home or something in it—a picture or a piece of furniture—or ask them what they think of some local happening or the latest flap in Washington.

For the first few dates, girls usually get off the hook as far as talking to boys' parents is concerned. If the relationship continues, however, you're bound to meet them. When you do, follow the same rules in talking to his mother and father that he should follow in talking to yours. You can't go wrong with ritual questions and answers, compliments, or comments on current events.

By now, you may have learned something about his parents' interests and can make some reference to them. "Andy tells me you have a new Honda. How do you like it?" Or, "I hear you're a golfer. How often do you play?"

It may take a long time to feel entirely comfortable with a boy friend's or girl friend's family, but that doesn't mean you can't talk to them pleasantly and politely. Most mothers and fathers are anxious to get acquainted with their children's dates. There's no reason why youngsters shouldn't feel the same way about their dates' parents.

One question that troubles a great many people who have never gone out on a date is: what will we say to each other?

Writer Laura Cunningham recently confessed in *The New York Times* that when she was thirteen years old she wrote in her diary: "I am convinced that people go all the way because they can't think of anything to say."

Cunningham was so afraid of going "all the way" that she drew up a list of topics and kept it next to the phone so she could jump in and start talking the instant a boy called to ask her out. On her first date she chattered compulsively all the way home from the movies and didn't once mention the weather—despite the fact that a torrential downpour with hurricane-force winds had sprung up while they were in the theater.

Whether you're hoping to head off a sexual invitation or are simply too nervous to shut up, one-sided conversations aren't advisable. Dates were designed to give people a chance to get to know each other. That means you each have to do your share of the talking.

What can you talk about? Ask the people you know who go out a lot what they talk about on dates. The answer will be anything and everything. There's no set formula, and, whether they're willing to admit it or not, their conversations are probably as full of awkward pauses and silences broken by both people talking at once as yours are.

A psychologist at Brown University recently arranged for a young man who was nervous about dating to observe the behavior of one of his more sociable classmates. "That guy's as bad as I am!" the observer exclaimed in amazement.

While you're getting organized for your date, think of some topics you might talk about. Do you take the same courses in school, watch the same TV shows, or listen to the same music? What kind of movies and books do you like? What do you do with your summers, or hope to do when you finish school?

Nervousness is inevitable on dates—especially first

dates. But don't forget that your date will be nervous, too. Instead of fretting about making a fool of yourself, turn your attention to making him feel at ease.

If you should say or do something foolish on a date, don't decide that all is lost. The woods are full of loving couples who survived all sorts of first-date embarrassments from tripping over their own feet on a dance floor to not having enough money to pay the tab.

It's only natural to feel depressed when a date doesn't go as well as you'd hoped. Or worse, when it goes fine, but he doesn't call back, or she's busy the next time you call her. It's as hard to understand why some male-female relationships don't click as it is to figure out why others do.

If a friendship for which you had high hopes fizzles, don't decide that you're unlovable or work yourself into a fit of jealousy at whomever takes your place. Pick up your fractured ego, put the pieces back together, and look around for somebody who'll be smart enough to realize what a terrific person you are.

8 | How to Say No

THERE was a story in the news not long ago about a group of Connecticut teenagers who were riding around one evening looking for something to do. One of them came up with the idea of challenging some friends to a drag race. Everyone went along with the plan except one young man who said, "No, thanks. Just drop me off at my corner. I'm going home."

Of the five people who were in the car that evening, the young man who got out and went home is the only one still alive and well. Three of the others are dead, and one will be in a wheelchair for the rest of his life.

In retrospect, the young man did the right thing, but it probably wasn't so simple and clear-cut at the time. It takes a lot of guts to say no. You run the risk of being laughed at, of looking like a goody-goody, of not being one of the gang.

Nevertheless, saying no can save your life—literally,

as it did in the case of the Connecticut teenager, or figuratively, in the sense that it takes your life out of other people's hands and makes it your own responsibility.

You may never think of your life as being in anyone else's hands, but that's exactly where it is when you regularly go along with things you don't want to do because other people expect it. If you can remember a few of the times when that happened, you may recall how emotionally confused you felt—vaguely irritated at whoever seemed to be pressuring you into saying yes, ashamed of yourself for saying it, and on top of all that, stymied because you didn't see how you could possibly say no.

That's where you were wrong. There are a few situations—they aren't too hard to recognize—in which your parents or teachers have some say, but aside from those, you're the one who's running the show.

Perhaps you've heard or read about Assertiveness Training, the program designed to help people take charge of their own lives. Its basic idea can be summed up in a single sentence: *You don't have to do what other people want or expect, and the easiest way not to do it is to say no.*

How do you learn to say that short, but oh-so-difficult, word? You must first realize that it can be said without sounding rude or abrupt. There's no need to raise your voice, lose your temper, or deliver a sermon on anyone else's behavior. Make it clear that you're saying no because it's right for you. What other people do, or how they react to what you do, is their business, not yours.

Psychologist Manuel J. Smith, who is one of the leaders in the field of Assertiveness Training, spells out another rule to remember when you're learning to say no: *You don't have to offer reasons or excuses to justify your behavior.*

Most of us feel apologetic about saying no and think we owe others some explanation for our decision. You can offer an explanation if you want to, but it's frequently better if you don't. If the other person dismisses your explanation or comes up with an argument against it, you're left with nothing to fall back on.

If you tell a salesperson, for example, that you can't buy the jacket you've been looking at because you don't have enough money with you, he may try to talk you into putting a deposit on it. Then where are you?

If you tell a friend that she can't borrow your roller skates because the laces are broken, she may say, "No problem. I have an extra pair." Again, you're stuck.

It's better to say to the salesperson, "No thanks. It's not what I had in mind," or "Thanks for your help, but I'd like to look a little bit more before I decide." And the friend who wants to borrow your skates can be told, "I'm sorry, I expect to be using them myself," or "I never lend things to people. I'm too afraid that something will happen to them," or "I lent them to you last week. Why don't you ask someone else this time?"

Don't elaborate on your explanation. Don't try to back it up with other excuses. And don't be swayed by anger, bullying, or ridicule. Hold your ground and repeat your original statement as often as it takes to make it sink in. If your resolve starts to crumble, remind yourself: *You don't have to do what other people want or expect, and the easiest way not to do it is to say no.*

It's impossible to list all the situations in which you may want to, or should, say no, but let's take a look at some of the most important ones. If you can learn to handle those, you're not likely to be thrown by the others.

On the Job

It's always difficult to say no to adults, especially when you're on their payroll. But if you work for somebody who consistently asks you to stay late, change your day off, or do jobs you weren't hired to do, you have every right to refuse.

Do it politely, of course. If it's a question of staying late, say, "I'm sorry. I have an important appointment, and I have to leave on time." Changing a day off can be handled with, "I'm sorry, I've already made plans for Wednesday, and they can't be changed."

Don't offer any further explanations, and stick to your guns no matter how hard your boss tries to dissuade you.

If the person you work for has a habit of asking you if you'd mind doing a substantial amount of extra work without any extra pay, you can reply that yes, you're afraid you do mind. Point out that you were hired to do baby-sitting, not housework, or to mow the lawn, not trim the hedges. Say that you think you're doing a good job in other respects and you hope he or she thinks so, too, but you're much too busy with your regular chores to take on any more. Another alternative is to ask if there's been a change in your duties. If so, perhaps you should discuss a change in your pay as well.

When you have to bring these matters to the attention of an employer, do it in a businesslike way. Look him in the eye, be firm but not hostile, and don't resort to whining, sulkiness, or insults. You're not out to give your employer a hard time; you simply want to stop him from giving you one.

Eating

Another situation in which adults tend to push kids around —often without realizing it—is eating. You can usually fight off your own mother, but it isn't so easy with somebody else's. Nevertheless, if you're stuffed, or on a diet, or don't like the food all that much, you have the right to say, "No, thank you." The dictates of your stomach take precedence over the goodwill of your host or hostess.

If you're dieting, you'd be smarter not to mention it. A distressing number of people see no harm in sabotaging other people's attempts to lose weight. Some of them actually think they're doing you a favor. "Just this once won't hurt," or "You're fine the way you are," they say as they pile another helping on your plate.

If anyone seems determined to make you eat more than you want or need, skip the explanation. Head your hostess off with a polite but definite, "It's delicious, but I really don't care for any more." Keep saying it as often as you have to, and if you still find yourself staring at a second helping, you're not under any obligation to eat it.

Drinking

If someone offers you a drink of beer, wine, or whiskey, there's no law that says you have to take it—even if you're the only one not drinking. You can say, "No thanks, I'd rather have a soft drink." If soft drinks aren't being served, "Sorry, I don't drink," will do.

If people tease you about not drinking, let them. Deciding when, whether, what, and how much to drink is a highly personal matter. You also have to give some serious consideration to the consequences. If you're under-age, you could run afoul of the law. No matter how old you are, you should know that thousands of people are killed or maimed in motor vehicle and other types of accidents each year and that the majority of those accidents are related to the use of alcohol.

Alcohol on its own can do a great deal of damage to the human body. It's also addictive for certain people, which means that when you start drinking, there's a chance you may become one of the nine million Americans who can't stop.

Even if you don't drink, you may find yourself in a car driven by someone who does. If he's had too much, try to talk him out of getting behind the wheel: "I think you've had one too many. Why don't you let someone else drive?" or "Why don't I call home and get my father to pick us up?"

If he refuses, don't, under any circumstances, get in the car yourself. Find a phone and call someone—a parent, a friend, the nearest taxi company—to take you home. Don't hesitate for fear your folks will find out that you've been drinking, too. They may be furious, but when they calm down, they'll be grateful that you had the good sense to admit that you didn't belong on the highway and to turn to them for help.

Sex

Sexual invitations are usually thought of as a girl's problem, but boys occasionally find themselves being manipulated into proving their masculinity or their sophistication. Such invitations can be difficult to deal with. Keep in mind, however, that sex should never be used to prove anything; nor should it be seen as a source of attention, adventure, pleasure, or popularity without any regard for your own or your partner's true feelings.

You should know, if you don't already, that every act of sexual intercourse has the potentiality for creating a new life. Don't ever "take a chance," "get carried away," or "do it just this once," because you don't have the courage to say no.

If someone you like does the asking, your greatest fear may be that you'll never see him again if you refuse. If that happens, it's a sure sign that he wasn't interested in you as a person—only as a conquest. No matter how dreamy he is, you're better off without him.

The easiest way to turn down a sexual invitation is to tell the other person how you feel. Say, "I'm sorry. I like you very much, but I don't feel ready for that kind of relationship," or "It would make me feel guilty and I don't want to feel that way," or "I'd rather wait until I feel right about it."

There's no arguing with somebody else's feelings. They're much too personal to be criticized or changed. If you're honest about expressing yours, your date will have to respect them, even if he doesn't like them. A boy who cares about you in the right way should value the fact that you're willing to tell him how you feel.

If you're not interested in a date in a sexual way, it's only fair to let him know where he stands. Let him down gently: "I like you and I enjoy your company, but I'm not really attracted to you in that way."

Nobody likes to be rejected, so when you turn down a sexual invitation, be sure to soften your refusal with, "I'm sorry," or "Please don't be hurt." Unless your date has been crude or presumptuous, don't act huffy or moralistic. You may have done something to make him think he could ask.

Many couples—even married ones—use sex as a substitute for other forms of communication. Don't let that happen to you. When you're out with your boy friend or girl friend, keep the conversation going. Your relationship will be much stronger if you can learn to be intimate on a mental or emotional level. If you really care about each other you should be able to share:

- a belief that's important to you
- a story in which you come off looking bad
- a significant event from your past
- your worst fear
- your dreams for the future

If neither of you feels ready to reveal these things, you're not ready for physical intimacy either. Give your relationship time to mature and yourselves time to decide how serious it is. If you're wise, you'll keep on saying no until you're sure.

Law Breaking

There are any number of things some kids do for kicks—using drugs, shoplifting, reckless driving, vandalism—that are in violation of the law. It's easy to shrug and tell yourself everyone does it, but if you're really in charge of your own life, you don't do things because everyone else does them. You do them because you think they're right for you. When you don't think so, you say "I'll see you guys later. I'm going home."

Once you stop going along with the gang, you may be surprised to discover the gang going along with you. Some of your friends who aren't brave enough to say no themselves may be looking for someone to say it for them. If you lead the way with, "Count me out," or "Not for me," you may hear a few of your pals chiming in with, "Me, too."

You can't count on that happening, of course. It's difficult to predict how people will react to a person who goes his own way. Some of your friends may feel threatened by your independence and give you a hard time; others may be more or less indifferent to it. Either way, you know you're doing the right thing, and that's what counts.

9 | Formal Occasions

IF there's any occasion that's guaranteed to bring on a case of the shys, it's a formal gathering—a wedding, funeral, or anniversary party, for instance, or a dress-up dinner at a restaurant or somebody else's home.

Guests at such functions have been known to become so befuddled that they've shaken hands with head-waiters, congratulated funeral directors, and extended condolences to brides. Some have gone without salt, pepper, or butter because they were too shy to ask for them, and opera star Cornell MacNeil once passed up the Rock Cornish game hen at a black-tie banquet because he was afraid it would slide off his plate when he tried to cut it.

There's no question that formal affairs intimidate anyone who isn't used to them—and that includes not only kids but a great many adults as well. The main reason is that formal functions usually take place in unfamiliar surroundings and involve large groups of people. The larger the crowd and the less familiar the setting, the more unglued most of us become.

If you haven't attended enough formal gatherings to know what to expect, do some homework the next time you're going to one. Ask your parents, or anyone you know who's been to a similar affair, what goes on. Supplement their comments by reading a book of etiquette. If you don't have one at home, you can find one in the library.

A good etiquette book will give you enough information to keep you from feeling completely at sea. Although not every function is run precisely "by the book" the basic ingredients are usually the same; and the rituals for religious ceremonies like weddings, christenings, Bar Mitzvahs, and funerals rarely vary.

Unless you're among the participants in a formal ceremony, there's not much you have to do except show up and be courteous, or, as someone said about acting, "Know your lines, and don't bump into the furniture."

If your invitation to the affair includes an R.S.V.P., have the good manners to reply promptly. A hostess has to know how many guests to plan for. Unless there's a first-class emergency, such as illness or a death in your family, don't ever back out of an invitation you've accepted. By the same token, once you've refused an invitation, don't call back to say that you can come after all.

If you're extremely close to whomever is giving the party and have a good excuse for changing your plans, you might risk it. If you do, be profuse in your apologies, and leave the door open for your hostess to say no. Say something like, "This is terribly rude of me, but I just found out that we're not going to visit my grandmother in Florida after all. I'd like to come to the wedding (or dinner or party), but if it's going to be inconvenient for you, please say so. I'll understand."

If your hostess says that it's impossible to include another guest at this late date, don't argue or act hurt. She'll feel as badly about the situation as you do, so be quick to assure her that it's quite all right, you honestly do understand.

The things people talk about on formal occasions aren't much different from the things they talk about on informal ones. There are certain ritual remarks and conduct that are appropriate for specific functions, however. You won't be so anxious about your behavior if you know in advance what they are.

Weddings

You'll have one less thing to feel self-conscious about if you show up wearing the right clothes. Women guests at a wedding never wear white so as not to compete with the bride. Otherwise, best dress is the rule, although the degree of dressiness will depend on the time of day. Save your extra-fancy clothes for evening weddings. Sequins, satins, and sparkly jewelry are out of place in the daytime. If you're in doubt, check with some of the other guests, or call the bride's mother. Even if you don't know her, she should recognize your name from the invitation list. She'll be happy to give you some guidance.

If it's a church wedding, there'll be ushers to escort people to their pews. If you're with your parents, the usher will probably offer your mother his arm and let you follow behind. If you arrive on your own, you'll get your own usher. Tell him whether you're a friend or relative of the bride or groom so he'll know which side of the church to seat you on (the bride's guests sit on the left) and how close to the altar you should be.

Don't worry about what to say as the usher escorts you up the aisle. He's probably thought up a few remarks for the occasion. If he's as unsure of himself as you are, however, try something simple: "Isn't this a beautiful day?" or "What a nice church!" By the time he agrees with you, you'll be at your pew.

There isn't much you have to do during the wedding ceremony, except pay attention. If it's a Catholic wedding with a nuptial mass, however, there'll be a point about midway in the service where the priest will ask the congregation to offer one another the sign of peace. This is your cue to shake hands and say, "Peace be with you," to the people on either side of you or in the pews nearby.

After the wedding and before the reception, there'll be a receiving line consisting of the bride and groom,

their mothers and sometimes their fathers, and their at-
tendants. Step up to the person at the head of the line—
usually the bride's mother—and offer her your hand. If
you don't know her, or aren't sure she'll remember you,
introduce yourself and add a word or two of identification.
"I'm Jim Turner, Peter's first cousin," or "I'm Ann Davis;
Connie was my favorite counselor at camp."

Follow that up with a sentence or two about the
occasion: "What a beautiful wedding," "Isn't this a happy
day?" or "Don't Connie and Peter make a wonderful
pair?"

You can say pretty much the same thing to everyone
on the receiving line, omitting the introductions, of course,
with people you already know. Keep your remarks concise. This is no time for lengthy exchanges. There are
other guests to be greeted, and it isn't fair to hold up the
line.

It's customary to kiss the bride, but if you feel un-
easy about social kissing, no one will mind if you shake
her hand. Tell her she looks beautiful, and wish her every
happiness, but offer congratulations only to the groom.
Congratulating the bride makes it sound as if she's scored
a victory by landing a husband.

If you don't know anybody at the wedding except the
bride or groom and their families—who may be too busy
to talk to you—don't hesitate to introduce yourself to the
other guests. Do it just as you did on the receiving line
and say, "I don't know very many people here." Weddings

are congenial occasions, and you'll soon find someone to talk to, especially since the setting of the wedding ceremony and the reception, and the appearance of the bride and groom will give you a built-in list of conversation starters.

Funerals

Paying a condolence call is a task few people relish. Other people's grief makes all of us uncomfortable. The prospect will be even less appealing if you've never done it before. You may be inclined to pretend you're busy and send a note or a sympathy card instead. Don't. Your presence will mean a great deal to the bereaved family, and if the person who died was a friend or a close relative of a friend—a parent, brother, or sister, for instance—you would be remiss if you failed to appear.

There's no need to wear black for the occasion, but don't show up in tight red pants or a glittery shirt either. Choose something on the quiet side. If the family is receiving visitors at a funeral home—as most families do these days—there'll be a bulletin board or someone stationed near the door to direct you to the proper room.

When you enter, go up to the member of the family you know best and say, "I'm so sorry." If there's a large crowd, you may not have a chance to say much more than that. If you do have time to talk, you can ask—if you don't know—if the death was sudden, how the family is bearing up, and when and where the funeral service and burial will be.

If you don't see any familiar faces, you'll have to extend your condolences to whomever is on hand. Usually, one person keeps an eye out for arriving visitors. He or she may step forward to greet you. Otherwise, pick out the person who seems most likely to be a member of the immediate family. Introduce yourself, and explain how you know the family; for example, "I'm a friend of Kathy's from school." Then say, "I'm so sorry."

The person you speak to will respond with some suitable remark and may introduce you to other family members. "I'm sorry to meet you under such sad circumstances," is the appropriate thing to say.

If there's a kneeling bench in front of the casket, you may want to kneel and say a short prayer. There may also be a funeral register either at the kneeling bench or near the door. Sign your full name before you leave so the family will have a record of your visit.

Funeral visits don't have to last more than ten or fifteen minutes, but if you're a close friend, you might want to—and probably should—stay longer. If you meet someone you know, it's all right to sit and talk for a while. Don't feel that you have to confine your conversation to the funeral or the deceased, but do keep your voice subdued, and be sure to make at least one ritual remark about the occasion: "Isn't it too bad?" or "I was so sorry to hear about so-and-so's death."

If the person who died is someone your own age, you probably remember some nice things about him. His family would like to hear them, but they'll probably be too devastated to handle such a discussion at the funeral. Put your memories in a letter that they can read in private and save.

Formal Meals

The main difference between formal meals and informal ones is that the food, the service, and the table decorations are fancier, and the guests are more dressed up and more likely to be on their best behavior. If you're not sure what your best behavior should be, it's time for another expedition into the etiquette book. In the meantime, here are a few rudimentary tips about table manners:

• Don't start eating the instant you sit down. Wait until your hostess picks up her fork or—at a public dinner—to see if an invocation will be said.

• Don't get in a tizzy over which fork to use. If the table is set properly, you simply start with the implements farthest from your plate and work your way in. There may be a fork and spoon placed horizontally in front of your plate; they're for dessert. The spoon goes in the right hand, the fork in the left—or vice versa if you're a lefty.

• If you need something that's halfway down the table, don't reach; ask someone to pass it to you. Say, "Excuse me," to get their attention, then, "May I have the butter please?"

• If you're served something you don't like, there's no need to explain that you hate it; just leave it on your plate. Similarly, if someone offers you a dish you don't like, simply say, "No, thank you."

Your primary duty as a guest at a formal meal is to be good company. Spend some time talking to the people on either side of you. If they're occupied, talk to the person sitting opposite you. If the table is too wide or he's already engaged in another conversation, feel free to listen in on—or join—any of the conversations around you.

The one thing you must never forget to say after a formal lunch or dinner—or after any other kind of party —is thank you. Your hostess has undoubtedly gone to a considerable amount of trouble and expense to entertain you, so don't hesitate to be profuse in your thanks. Tell her what a fine time you had, how delicious the food was, and how kind she was to ask you.

Funerals, weddings, and dress-up dinners are the most frequent social events. There are dozens of others, from debutante balls to formal teas. If you're invited to any of them, don't beg off because you're not sure how to behave. It won't take much effort to find out. Failing that, you can always follow somebody else's lead.

Formal gatherings are rarely as formidable as they seem. Whoever does the inviting usually makes a special effort to see that everyone feels welcome. You can do your part by making them feel they've succeeded.

Look your best, show up with an adequate supply of conversation-starters and topics to talk about, and don't lose track of the fact that, except in the case of funerals, you're there to have a good time.

10 | Interviews

INTERVIEWS are more harrowing than other forms of conversation because you know for a fact that you're being judged, and you also know that you can be rejected. If you're applying for a job or trying to get into a high-powered college or prep school, there's no way you can avoid being interviewed, but you can avoid doing poorly at it.

When Judge Sandra Day O'Connor appeared before the Senate Committee that was studying her qualifications for the job of associate justice of the United States Supreme Court, she offered a good lesson in how to behave at an interview. She looked alert and interested as she leaned forward in her seat and listened attentively to the difficult, often rambling, questions the senators put to her. Her answers were thoughtful but concise. They left no doubt that she had considered rather carefully what might be asked and had decided in advance how specific her answers would be.

If you're going to be interviewed for a job or a school, profit by Judge O'Connor's example. Give some thought to the questions that will be asked, and prepare the kind of answers that will put you in a favorable light.

Job Interviews

Nobody hires anyone for any kind of a job without an interview. Before you set out for an interview, think about what your prospective employer expects to discover from the meeting. The interview won't show him how well you work, but it will give him an idea of how you handle yourself, how you respond to other people, whether you're punctual and make a good appearance, and how interested you are in the job.

You'll be nervous, of course. If you're afraid your nervousness will ruin your chances, say so at the outset: "I'm always a little nervous when I'm applying for a job. I hope it won't interfere with this interview."

Laying your cards on the table will help allay your anxiety and, rather than counting against you, may actually win you points for being straightforward.

In a job interview, the interviewer asks most of the questions. Your job is to supply the answers. Before you rush to answer a question, however, make sure you know exactly what's being asked. If you have any doubts, say, "I'm afraid I don't understand your question."

Keep your answers brief. If you're not sure you've

supplied enough details, ask the interviewer if he wants to know more.

Don't bluff. Be honest about what you can do. You could be fired as soon as you're hired if you claim to have skills you don't possess.

If the interviewer points out a shortcoming, admit it, but don't put yourself down for it. If he remarks that you're young, for instance, say, "I'm sixteen" (not *only* sixteen), "but I think you'll find me mature for my age."

If the shortcoming can be corrected, say so. "No, I don't have a driver's license, but I expect to take the test in June."

If you don't see what bearing it has on the job, say that too—but in a nice way. "No, I don't type. Your ad didn't mention typing."

Respond only to what's asked. Don't volunteer information that's not relevant or casts doubts on your capabilities.

Sometimes an interviewer will ask a question that touches on a sore point. Don't rush in with explanations and admissions of failure. If he notes that you've never worked before, there's no need to go into the whole story of how you tried to find a job last summer but couldn't, or how you found one but hated it and quit in two days. It's sufficient to say, "I don't have any experience, but I think you'll find me a good worker. If you give me a chance, I know I can do the job."

Try to put everything you say in this same kind of positive light. Avoid negatives of any kind. Don't bad-mouth a present or previous employer, and don't complain about school, the weather, or the fact that the interviewer has kept you waiting or asked you to fill out ten million forms.

Some interviewers don't ask specific questions. Instead, they throw the ball to you saying, "Tell me about yourself." If that happens, there's no need to go into your whole life story. Give such pertinent details as your age, your school and grade, what skills you have for this particular job, any previous working experience. Don't forget to mention such personal qualities as intelligence, honesty, reliability, and willingness to work hard.

At some point in the interview—usually near the end—the interviewer will ask if you have any questions. This is when you can—in fact, should—inquire about the salary, the hours, and, if it's a permanent job, the possibilities for advancement. Not doing so will make you seem lackadaisical. Unless it's vital for you to know, questions about raises and time off can wait. If you really want the job, it's better to emphasize not what you stand to gain from it, but what the employer will gain from hiring you.

The interviewer will let you know when the meeting is over. He'll say something like, "I'm glad you were able to come see me," or "I'll call you when I've made up my mind." Be on the alert for such signals, and take your leave promptly.

Your good-bye should include a positive statement of your interest in the job. Don't say, "I really need this job," even if you do. Mention instead that you've always admired this particular company or been interested in this type of work. Close with, "I know I can do a good job. I hope you'll give me a chance to prove it."

School Interviews

Prep school and college admissions depend on a number of factors besides an interview, so unless you act like a real turkey, you won't be rejected on that basis alone. On the other hand, if your marks and board scores are less than spectacular, a good interview could tip the balance in your favor.

The more interviews you have, the less threatening they become. If possible, schedule your first interview at the school you least want to attend, and save the one you have your heart set on until last. By then, you should be better versed in the art.

The rules for prep school and college admissions interviews are much the same. If you're bright enough to be applying to either one, you shouldn't have to be told to study the catalogue—and whatever other material the school sends you—before your interview. You'll look like a dummy if you ask about something you should already know.

A school interview is a fairly formal occasion, so wear something better than your everyday school clothes. The college admissions adviser at one of New York City's private day schools recommends a sport coat, shirt, tie or sweater, and slacks for boys and a skirt, blouse, and blazer for girls.

Plan to arrive on campus at least fifteen minutes early so you and your parents—if they're with you—will have time to find the admissions office and collect your wits before going in. When you give your name to the receptionist, ask her whom you'll be seeing. Knowing the interviewer's name beforehand will cut down on your worries about not getting it straight when you meet.

You may be able to check out your interviewer in the school catalogue. You should have one with you, but if you don't, there'll probably be a copy in the waiting room. It might help to know his field of study and where he got his degrees. If he went to the same college your mother did, that would be an instant talking point. (Don't hesitate to say you noticed it in the catalogue; it will show how observant you are.) If the catalogue also mentions that he teaches calculus, you can tiptoe around the fact that you're allergic to all forms of math.

Actually, you shouldn't make negative comments about your courses, teachers, or anything else. Running things down makes you—not them—look bad.

Admissions interviewers usually ask a few standard questions, such as:

What do you think you can offer this school?
What do you consider your greatest strengths/ weaknesses?

What are your interests outside of school?

What book have you read recently that made a strong impression on you?

Come prepared with some intelligent answers to these questions. Give some thought, too, to the personal qualities, interests, and accomplishments you'd like to stress. You don't want to sound like a braggart, but this is no time to be modest either. Instead of making blunt statements about your strong points—except in answer to specific questions, of course—try to put them in a larger context. Tell what playing varsity basketball taught you about teamwork, or what insights your summer internship in Washington gave you into government.

Whenever possible, dovetail your interests with something the school has to offer; for example, "I see you offer a major in Russian Studies. I took a course in Russian history last semester, and I really enjoyed it."

Be prepared to back up your statement with something specific that intrigued you—Peter the Great, the power of the czars, the events that led up to the revolution.

If the interviewer asks about your career plans or what you expect to major in, don't be vague. If you can't give a definite answer, pick out an area that interests you. A reply like, "I'm thinking of majoring in economics," or "I'm leaning toward a career in science," will show that you have some sense of direction.

If you don't understand a question, say, "Excuse me,

I'm not sure I understand your question." If you understand but don't have an answer on the tip of your tongue, say, "I'm not quite sure how to answer that." This will give you a second or two to assemble your thoughts and take a stab at it.

Be sure to come armed with a few questions of your own. What about geographical and ethnic diversity? Financial aid? Year abroad? Work-study programs?

Another good question: "What are my chances of getting into this school?" The interviewer should be able to give you a fairly good assessment based on your academic record and his knowledge of the admissions standards. There's no point in putting any further time or energy into applying if you're certain to be rejected.

Admissions interviews last anywhere from thirty minutes to an hour. The interviewer will signal when it's time to leave. You can close with a polite statement like, "I enjoyed talking to you," or "This interview has been very helpful," or, if it seems more appropriate, a simple, "Good-bye, Mr., Mrs., Miss, or Ms. _____. Thank you very much."

After the interview, take a few minutes to critique your performance. Don't give yourself a hard time for not being more articulate. Admissions interviewers don't expect young people to be overly glib. But see if there's any question for which you should be better prepared the next time around, any point you might have stressed but didn't.

If this is your final interview, forget about a critique. You did your best. The rest is up to the admissions committee.

People who are being interviewed tend to forget that it's a two-way process. You're evaluating the interviewer—and the job or the school—just as much as they're evaluating you. Keep your eyes and ears open. Don't be afraid to ask questions. If you come away with an unfavorable impression or a feeling that the place isn't right for you, apply somewhere else.

11 | Audience Anxiety

PRESIDENT John F. Kennedy once asked Theodore Roosevelt's daughter, Alice Longworth, if she would care to say a few words at a White House ceremony honoring her father. Mrs. Longworth, who hated to speak in public, replied with a very few words: "No, thank you."

Wouldn't it be nice if you could say the same thing the next time you're called on to read or recite in class or make an announcement at a school assembly?

Some people don't mind speaking in public. A few unself-conscious types actually enjoy it. But it scares the life out of most people. Doctors who studied the heart rates of one group of speechmakers discovered that on the average they jumped from a normal rate of about 80 beats per minute to 114 beats just prior to the subjects' speeches to a high of 124 when they started to talk.

You've undoubtedly detected an increase in your

own heartbeat whenever you've had to speak before a group. Fortunately, you're the only one who notices that; but if you don't get your anxieties under control, your audience will be aware of your fearful look, rapidly shifting eyes, pale complexion, and shaky voice. And that's only for starters. You may also find yourself stammering, groping for words, not being able to remember simple facts—in all, proving the old saying, "The human brain is a wonderful thing. It starts working the moment you are born and never stops until you stand up to speak in public."

Psychologist Arnold H. Buss has pinpointed some of the major causes of audience anxiety—the term he uses to describe what happens to people who are terrified of speaking before a group. One is the feeling that you're conspicuous. Another is the novelty of the experience—you're not used to it—and of the perspective—people look different when you're on your feet looking out at them. Another anxiety component is the audience you're addressing. The larger, the more prestigious, the less familiar, the less attentive, and the less like yourself they are, the more frightened you'll be.

George Bernard Shaw was an excellent public speaker. When someone asked him how he mastered the art, the playwright replied, "I did it the same way I learned to skate—by doggedly making a fool of myself until I got used to it."

You should make an effort to get used to public speaking. It's a skill that will come in handy not only now, while you're still in school, but later on in life, when you may be called on to give a business report, deliver a eulogy, propose a toast, or preside over the PTA.

If you do have to speak, don't just grit your teeth and pray that you won't make too big a fool of yourself. Even if you're positive that this is the one and only time you're ever going to speak in public, think of it as practice, and try to do it right. You'll feel better. Your audience will be more receptive (you may even collect a few compliments), and you'll also discover that public speaking—while it may never become your favorite pastime—isn't quite as grisly as you imagined.

What Are You Going to Say?

Mark Twain said, "It usually takes more than three weeks to prepare a good impromptu speech." He may have been exaggerating, but he wasn't wrong in noting that even a short and simple talk requires quite a bit of planning. What you decide to say will depend to a large extent on whether you're out to entertain, inform, or persuade your audience. You may hope to do all three, but one will still be more important than the others. That's the one to emphasize.

If you're asking your classmates to donate to UNICEF, for instance, don't spend all your time talking about the organization and tack your request for money on at the end. Tell them right off the bat that you're looking for contributions. Spell out some good reasons why they should give, and offer some suggestions on how they can earn the money to do it. You can't omit talking about the organization entirely, but if you expect to get results, your main thrust will be *giving* to the organization.

Once you know which direction your talk will take, your next task is to point it in that direction and move it along at a snappy pace. Even a talk on an assigned topic —something as uninspiring as the federal budget—can be livened up if you take a creative approach. Pick out one or two startling facts or statistics, and look for anecdotes, personalities, and specific details that will make your material come alive.

Never talk any longer than your allotted time. Clock yourself in advance to be sure you're hitting the mark. The rule of thumb professionals use is that one triple-spaced typewritten page equals one minute of talking. (If you're writing in longhand, that's about 150 words.) Triple-spacing, incidentally, makes a speech easier to follow when you're on your feet and gives you room to write in any last-minute corrections.

Stay away from fancy words, roundabout sentences, and vague ideas. Say what you have to say clearly and concretely. Talk as you would if you were addressing a group of people gathered in your living room.

Should You Write Out Your Speech in Advance?

There are two schools of thought about how to prepare a speech. Some speakers feel more secure if they write out exactly what they want to say. The only trouble is that they often insist on reading it. This destroys all sense of spontaneity. For one thing, it requires looking at your script instead of at the people you're talking to. For another, it tends to make you rush to get to the end of sentences, paragraphs, and pages without giving much thought to what the words mean or where the emphasis should be placed.

The majority of speech coaches advise their students not to use a prepared script but to talk from notes instead. The notes outline the main points which the speaker can go on to discuss in his own words.

This is an excellent way to deal with introductions, announcements, and similarly brief speeches. If you're an inexperienced speaker and you have to talk for more than five minutes, however, you may be too frightened to carry it off. Until you become accustomed to speaking on your feet or have the occasion to talk about something you're familiar with, it's safer to write out your speech in advance. Go over it with a red pencil or felt-tipped pen. Underline the words that should be emphasized, and make vertical lines at the places where you should pause. If there are words you find hard to pronounce, write them out phonetically or underline the syllables you should accent. Better still, find synonyms that will be easier to say.

Read your speech over several times before you give it. You should be familiar enough with the material so you can look out at your audience from time to time without losing track of where you are.

Whatever you do, though, don't memorize your

talk. It will come out sounding as boring and sing-songy as the multiplication tables. Worse yet, if your mind goes blank in the middle of it, you'll have to go all the way back to the beginning to find out what comes next.

Don't Hold Your Breath

Some speakers take a deep breath at the beginning of a speech and keep on talking until they're forced to come up for air. By then, their voices are so weak that they can barely be heard.

Take a few deep breaths before you stand up to help calm your nerves. Then inhale and exhale at a regular pace so you'll have enough air to project your voice. Time your breathing so when you do have to pause, you'll do it at a logical point in your talk. Pauses are a definite plus. They give your listeners a chance to absorb what you've been saying, and they make you seem more authoritative. The speaker who can tolerate a few seconds of silence comes across as much more in control of his subject and his audience than the speaker who rattles on like a runaway train.

How Serious Should You Be?

If you're not a natural humorist, don't feel you have to tell a funny story to warm up your audience. Most of the jokes that are recommended for this purpose are hackneyed; even people who are good at joke-telling would be wise to avoid them.

That doesn't mean that speaking in public has to be dull, however. Serious subjects can frequently be handled with a light touch. If that won't work, keep your voice upbeat and peppy so your audience will see that you're fired up about what you're saying. It may persuade them to get fired up, too.

Although humor isn't essential in a good speech, it helps. If you have an amused outlook on life and you're good at conveying it, don't hesitate to capitalize on your gifts. Stay away from prepackaged material, however, and be careful of overkill. Use something original and personal—an incident you were involved in, a remark you overheard, an insight that's uniquely yours. Remember not to make your story too long and complicated, and be sure it suits both the audience and the occasion.

Where Should You Put Your Hands?

If you're nervous—and you will be—your hands are one of the giveaways. You should keep them occupied so you won't start fiddling with your hair, clothes, or jewelry. If you have a written-out speech, you can hold on to that. If you're talking from notes, use 4 x 6 index cards; they're a good size to grasp and easier to see as well.

If what you say is impromptu—reciting in class or speaking up at a meeting, for instance—use a pencil, pen, or ruler for a prop. People who wear reading glasses find these effective, too. Whatever you choose, hold it still, except for an occasional gesture when you're making a point. Remember, too, to hold it above your waist so your listeners' attention will be directed to the upper half of your body—where your mouth is.

Stage Fright

Stage fright afflicts everyone who performs in public—even people who are used to it. Singer Carly Simon once got so rattled in the middle of a performance that she rushed off stage without singing any of her biggest hits.

There's no cure for stage fright, but you can make things a little easier on yourself if you prepare for your public. When you're going to stand up and speak, wear something you know you look good in. The day you give your first report as class treasurer isn't the day to experiment with a new outfit or hairdo.

Don't wait until the last minute to decide what you're going to say or to arrive at the place where you're going to say it. No matter how short your remarks will be, go over them a few times so you'll feel at home with the material. Before you go on, give yourself time to collect your thoughts and catch your breath, and to comb your hair and go to the bathroom, if necessary.

Your prespeech anxieties will seem trivial compared to the trauma you'll experience when you stand up and face your audience. Pause and take a deep breath. This is a good way to get your audience's attention and it also helps you relax. While you're doing it, look for two or three friendly faces in the crowd and address your talk to them. Select people sitting in different parts of the room so your eyes will move around and not be riveted to one spot.

You may be surprised at how intently people are watching you and how willing they are to give you their attention. In the beginning, at least, most audiences are on the speaker's side. They want to hear something new and interesting, and they may also be secretly glad that you're doing the talking, not them.

No matter how nervous you are, don't say anything about it. You'll lose your audience's respect, which is essential to keeping their attention. Stand tall, and act as though you do this sort of thing every day.

Speak slowly, even if it kills you. This will give you time to breathe, take some of the shakiness out of your voice, and make you easier to understand as well. If you stumble over a word or botch up a phrase, don't get flustered. Simply say it over again the right way.

Most amateur speakers would love to find something to hide behind. If that's how you feel, don't try to hide behind your notes; hide behind what's in them. Throw yourself into your subject. Get excited about it. Make your audience get excited too. If you concentrate on doing that, you'll be too busy to be afraid.

Actress Cornelia Otis Skinner was usually jittery before she went on stage, but she once confessed that she worried more about *not* being nervous. When she felt too relaxed, she maintained, she knew she wasn't keyed up to do her best. Professional athletes, musicians, and political candidates have said the same thing.

Dreadful as it is, stage fright isn't a bad thing to suffer from. A good part of the tension you feel is nature's way of helping you rise above your normal abilities, allowing you to do well in a crisis.

A wise man once said: Never stand up to speak in front of a group unless (1) you really want to, and (2) you absolutely have to. Few people really want to, but there will be times when you absolutely have to. Given a choice, don't be too quick to say, "No, thank you." Use the occasion to get some practice for the times when you can't back out.

12 | A Dozen Common Dilemmas and How to Deal with Them

1. Compliments

Most of us get embarrassed when people say nice things about us. Not that we don't like to hear them—it's just that we feel self-conscious when anyone calls attention to us. If you happen to have a low self-image, the problem goes deeper. You know, even if the person who compliments you doesn't, that you don't deserve such praise (which may only prove that you don't know as much as you think you do).

Deflecting a compliment—for whatever reason—isn't a very gracious thing to do. It can make the person who paid it—and was trying to be nice—feel as if he's said the wrong thing. The next time someone compliments you on what you're wearing, don't respond with, "This old thing? I can't stand it." If you're praised for being good at something, don't question the person's judgment or denigrate your abilities with a remark like, "I don't play tennis *that* well. You should see my brother."

Accept compliments in the spirit in which they're given, whether you think you deserve them or not. Respond with a smile and a, "Thank you," or "How nice of you to say so."

If you feel self-conscious, turn attention away from yourself by using the compliment as a kick-off for another conversation—which may be what the person who complimented you intended. A remark on something you're wearing, for instance, could be followed up with a few words about the color (is it one of your favorites?), the fabric (is it wrinkle-proof?), or where, when, or why you bought it.

A comment on your tennis game could prompt you to talk about your instructor, the courts you use, or another better-known player; for example, "I was watching John McEnroe on TV the other day. What do you think of that fierce temper of his?"

2. Introductions

Introducing people is one of the easiest things in the world to do, but most people tackle it with a certain amount of trepidation. Perhaps it's like the centipede who claimed he never had any trouble walking until people started asking him which foot went first. When he stopped to think about it, he got all mixed up.

The correct form is that younger people are introduced to older ones, average citizens are introduced to VIPs, and—if they're about equal in age and importance—men are introduced to women. Thus, you would say, "Mr. Owens, I'd like you to meet Jeff Scott," "Senator Condon, I'd like you to meet Mr. Owens," or "Judy, I'd like you to meet Jeff Scott."

Get in the habit of following these rules, but don't act as if you've committed a crime when you forget. It's more important to pronounce both people's names clearly and to add a few words of identification to make it easier for them to start a conversation if they want to. You could mention, for example, that Jeff just moved to your town from California and can't get used to your icy winters, that Mr. Owens is an avid fisherman, or that Judy is one of the stars of the school drama group.

When you're introduced to someone, you can respond with a formal, "How do you do?" although nowadays, "Hello," and, with your contemporaries, "Hi," are acceptable. If you're seated, stand up to be introduced—even to someone your own age. It's friendlier. A handshake, although not essential, is another friendly touch. Use a firm grip, don't squeeze too hard or hold on too long, and don't forget to smile.

Be sure to get the name of the person you're meeting. If you miss it the first time, ask to have it repeated. If you're still not sure, have him spell it out. He won't mind; he'll be glad you're that interested.

3. Forgetting Names

If you draw a blank on names when you have to introduce people, take heart, there's an easy way out. Acknowledge your problem, and throw yourself on the mercy of your friends. Most of them probably have the same trouble, so they can't afford to be critical. "In situations like this," you can say, "I can hardly remember my own name, so I hope you'll come to my rescue if I stumble over yours."

If you're introducing one person to a group, which is always tricky because you have to remember several names, you might say lightly—*not* apologetically—"This is my friend, Cindy. I'm not very good at introductions. Would you mind introducing yourselves?"

It's hard to object to that approach. Some people actually prefer it. It makes it easier for the newcomer to connect names with faces, and the people who are being introduced often feel better if they take an active, rather than a passive, role in the procedure.

It can be crushing when the shoe's on the other foot and somebody forgets your name. As one of the characters in John Irving's novel *The Hotel New Hampshire* observes, "In this world, just when you're trying to think of yourself as memorable, there is always someone who forgets that they've met you."

People who don't remember that you've already met seldom intend to be rude. Some of them have faulty memories; some only remember people they see all the time;

and some are so ill at ease in social situations that their brains get numb. Give them the benefit of the doubt, and be as merciful to them as you'd want them to be to you. Tell them your name in full, and if it doesn't seem to ring a bell, add some further identification, such as, "We met at Debbie Wallace's house," or "I used to be in your Boy Scout troop."

Don't ever put people on the spot by saying, "I'll bet you don't remember me," and forcing them to guess who you are. This trick is both embarrassing and irritating. Anyone who tries it deserves to wind up like the man who stumped a Texas congressman some years ago.

The man came up to the congressman at a political rally and said, "Hello, Congressman. We met a couple of years ago, but you probably don't remember me."

The congressman didn't, but he decided to try and bluff his way through. "Of course I remember you," he said heartily. "It's good to see you again."

"I'll bet you don't know my name," the man challenged him.

The congressman chuckled politely. "How could I forget it?" he asked. "How have you been?"

The man still wouldn't give up. "Congressman," he insisted, "you still haven't told me my name."

With that, the exasperated politician let out a roar. "Folks," he shouted, as everyone in the room turned in their direction, "is there anyone here who can tell this nincompoop who he is?"

4. Talking to the Handicapped

If you tend to shy away from people with handicaps because you're not sure how to act with them, the answer is: the same as you'd act with anyone else. Talk about the news, the weather, school, sports (which they may follow even if they can't play), or anything else that comes to mind.

Don't discuss, or, worse yet, ask questions about their handicaps, unless they bring them up. And do give some heed to how their handicap interferes with their functioning. It doesn't make sense to shout at a blind person as though he were deaf or treat someone in a wheelchair as if he's retarded.

If you think that a handicapped person can't cope with a particular situation, say quietly, "May I help you?" If the reply is yes, find out exactly how. Blind people generally prefer to take your arm rather than let you take theirs; people on crutches can usually get in and out of their coats or jackets but may need help opening doors.

Be sensitive to the fact that handicapped people are eager to be accepted as ordinary human beings. Don't ooze sympathy, don't feel you can't laugh or joke with them, and don't shower them with a lot of undue fussing that will only call attention to their plight.

5. Spills, Smashes, and Stumbles

Accidents happen in the best of families. Try to remember that old saying the next time you spill hot chocolate on somebody's sofa, knock over a lamp that looks suspiciously like a family heirloom, or stumble over a door sill that you should have seen but didn't.

Catastrophes of this sort make you feel awful. In some cases, even the magic words, "Forgive me," or "I'm sorry," can't repair the damage. The thoughtful host or hostess will try to ease your discomfort by assuring you that no serious damage has been done. If you suspect that isn't true, follow up your verbal apology with a written note. If you *know* it isn't true, offer to pay for cleaning, repairing, or replacing whatever you've damaged. If your offer is accepted, be quick about following through— even if you have to float a loan from your parents to do it.

Pratfalls are nightmarish because you not only look klutzy, you can hurt yourself besides. If you take a header, the first thing you should do is check carefully to be sure there's no damage. You'll feel silly if you assure everyone you're fine and then discover that you've sprained your ankle.

If you're not hurt, let everyone know at once so they can stop worrying. The old pun, "That was a nice trip. I think I'll go back next fall," is too corny. The other standby, "I always did have two left feet," isn't much better, but it will do in a pinch. If you're looking for something livelier, how about, "Don't mind me. I'm auditioning for a part in Cheech and Chong's new movie."

A smile will ease everyone's tensions, but if you can't think of an amusing remark, stick to a simple, "I'm sorry," or "How clumsy of me," and let it go at that.

Whatever type of disaster befalls you—a spill, smash, or stumble—don't spend the next two hours talking about the dopey thing you did. Apologize, help with the cleanup if one is necessary, and gloss it over as quickly as possible. Everyone else will be as eager to forget it as you are.

6. Wearing the Wrong Thing

If you've ever showed up somewhere in a T-shirt and patched jeans only to discover that everyone else was wearing good clothes, or put on your dressiest outfit and found the rest of the crowd in sneakers, you probably wanted to turn around and go home. However, there's rarely any need to bow out of a party because you've arrived in the wrong clothes.

If it will make you feel better, you can say you're on your way to, or from, someplace else and didn't have time to change. You can also follow the advice society folks used to give their offspring: Never complain; never explain. These days the rules about dress are fairly flexible anyway, so stop brooding about your booboo, pretend you're having a good time, and you soon will be.

If it's a formal occasion and you're afraid your hostess will be offended by your casual outfit, take her aside and tell her you're sorry, you seem to have gotten your signals confused. Unless she's the most uptight person in the world, she'll be quick to tell you it doesn't matter.

And it doesn't—to anyone but you. Once you turn your attention to someone besides yourself, your concern about not being properly dressed will soon fade away.

7. Asking for the Bathroom

There's no reason to feel ashamed of excusing yourself to go to the bathroom or of having to ask where it is. The elimination of body wastes is a normal physiological function, although unfortunately it has also been the subject of hundreds of tasteless—and childish—jokes.

If you're out in public, say, "Excuse me," and add, if you wish, "I'll be back in a minute." Most people will know where you're going, but if anyone is obtuse enough to ask, you can say, "I want to wash my hands (or freshen up)," or simply, "I have to use the bathroom."

If you're not sure where the rest rooms are, ask a waiter, an usher, the manager, or anyone else who'd be likely to know.

If you're in a private home, ask your host or hostess where the bathroom is. You may prefer to inquire discreetly, but you don't have to. If you have a pretty good idea of where the bathroom might be, you can seek it out on your own. A good host or hostess will point you in the right direction as you start to leave the room. If they don't, however, you'll be on your own. Some bathrooms are easy to find. Searching for others can send you bumbling into closets or heading down cellar stairs. So, if you don't know where you're going, by all means ask.

8. When You Feel Sick

If you don't feel well, try not to alarm or upset the people you're with. If you have to make a fast dash to the bathroom because of an upset stomach or an attack of diarrhea, don't go into the details when you return. Just say you don't feel well, you think you may be coming down with a virus, and go home as quickly and quietly as possible.

If you feel too sick to get home on your own, ask a friend to accompany you, or call home and get someone to pick you up. Lying down for a while sometimes helps, but most people prefer to be sick in their own beds. No matter how miserable you feel, don't carry on about it. It's not fair to let your indisposition spoil everyone else's fun.

9. Talking to Strangers

Anyone with any sense is leery of talking to strangers. However, if you're in a public place—a department store, coffee shop, waiting room, or elevator—and someone strikes up a conversation with you, it would be rude not to reply. In most cases, the people who start such conversations are only trying to be friendly. Some of them may be lonely, nervous, or bored.

This kind of conversation, usually called polite conversation, is undertaken without introductions. If someone does ask your name and address, you have reason to be suspicious. Change the subject (one way is by asking theirs instead), or make up an answer.

Polite conversations begin with ritual questions and rarely go much further. Your responses don't have to be lengthy. "Yes, it's a beautiful day," or "It *is* a long wait. This store (movie, dentist, etc.) seems to be very popular."

If you're not very talkative, you'll like one aspect of polite conversations: they're brief. When they aren't, it's up to the person who starts them to keep them going. All you have to do is provide perfunctory answers or nod and smile politely. You can indicate that you don't want to continue the conversation by looking away or—if the person is persistent—moving away. He or she will get the message and either stop talking or strike up a conversation with somebody else.

10. When Something Bugs You

If one of your friends persists in doing something that bugs you, the healthiest way to handle it is to say so. If you don't, you'll be doing yourself an injustice. What you'll be saying—unconsciously—is that your rights aren't important. That isn't true, but if you act as if it is, you'll spend a great deal of your time feeling angry both at yourself for being a doormat and at the rest of the world for treating you like one.

If you hate making a scene, you'll be relieved to know that you can air your grievances without shouting, hurling insults, or threatening anyone with violence. You can also do it without questioning the other person's motives or intentions, no matter how bad you think they are.

If someone is purposely being unfair to you, accusing

him of it will only force him to defend himself, and the point you're trying to make—which is to *please stop*—will get lost in the uproar. There's also the possibility that your accusation isn't justified. Some people are thoughtless out of carelessness, on the assumption that the other person won't notice or mind, or from a desire to save time and trouble for themselves.

Before talking about your dissatisfactions, make sure you have the other person's attention and that he's in the mood to listen. Open the discussion by saying, "There's something I want to talk to you about." Then spell out—in even tones—whatever it is that's bothering you: "I don't like those nasty cracks you keep making about my weight," or "I'm tired of lending you money all the time. Why don't you start carrying some of your own?"

Tell the other person how his actions make you feel—angry, embarrassed, hurt, taken advantage of—and ask him not to do it any more.

Nobody likes to hear criticism of themselves, so don't be surprised if your friend is angry or insulted at first. Tell him you don't want to hurt his feelings, but you think it's important for him to understand yours. If he counters by criticizing you, admit that you may be at fault, but suggest that you discuss his complaints some other time. Right now you're talking about *yours.*

If the disagreement involves some area of responsibility, like who's going to clean up after a party or how to divide up the chores on a camping trip, be willing to listen to the other person's point of view and to compromise. There must be some way to settle the matter so neither of you feels cheated.

Be sure to end your discussion on a friendly note. Get things back on an even keel by saying, "I'm sorry to have to talk to you like this, but it's something I felt you should know. I hope it won't interfere with our friendship."

A true friend may not like what you say, but he should appreciate your honesty in saying it. It means that you care about him enough not to want any hidden resentments between you.

The same ground rules apply when you want to complain about something to a parent, teacher, or employer:

1. Explain what's bothering you.
2. Tell how it makes you feel.
3. Suggest something the other person can do about it.
4. Be willing to listen to his point of view.
5. Don't get sidetracked by other issues or arguments.
6. End the discussion on a friendly note.

If you have a grievance against a store about something you bought, the rules are somewhat different. Tell the storeowner or salesperson what the problem is, for example, "This radio doesn't work," and what you expect to be done about it: "I want my money back," "I want another one," "Can you repair it?"

Have your sales slip with you. If you don't have one, know when you bought the item, how much you paid for it, and, if possible, be able to describe or point out the person who sold it to you.

Reputable stores are quick to honor legitimate complaints. If the one you're dealing with is less than reputable, you may have to withstand a barrage of defenses.

Be prepared to respond with an emphatic *no* if the salesman suggests that it's your fault, you must have dropped the radio on the way home or put the batteries in wrong. Don't be dissuaded by another ploy—trying to get rid of you by announcing that there are other people who need to be waited on. Remind him that you're a customer too.

You should come armed to a confrontation of this sort with a statement of what you'll do if your complaint isn't honored: report the store to the nearest consumer action agency, file a complaint in small claims court, tell everyone you know not to trade there, put your case in the hands of your uncle, the lawyer. Choose one, say it as if you meant it, and keep saying it no matter what excuses or accusations the storekeeper tries to make.

If the first person you talk to won't help, insist on seeing his boss, and say the same thing, just as emphatically, to him. If the boss is out, ask when he'll be back and say, "I'll be in to see him then."

Unless you're dealing with an outright crook, you should get some satisfaction—maybe not a refund (although it won't hurt to ask), but a credit or an offer to repair or replace the defective merchandise. If you don't, follow through on your threat to take further action.

11. Breaking Bad News

There are all kinds and degrees of bad news. You forgot to show up for a dentist appointment. You flunked geometry. You backed up without looking and tore the bumper off your father's car.

Whatever happened—and no matter how fervently you wish it hadn't—sooner or later you've got to tell the truth and take the consequences. It will be easier on everyone, including yourself, if you make it sooner.

When things go wrong and you're the one who's goofed, don't try to worm your way out of it. Don't tell lies, make complicated—and usually not very convincing —excuses, or try to blame someone else. Tell whomever needs to be told what happened. Say that you know it's your fault, tell them how awful you feel and how sorry you are, and ask if there's anything you can do to make amends.

Don't expect the other person not to be upset. Adults have emotions too. But it's worth an angry scene to have your misdeed out in the open and a remedy in the works.

If you're in serious trouble—you think you may be pregnant or you've been caught using drugs in school— trust your parents with the truth. They won't like it, but they'll appreciate hearing the story from you and not from someone else. After they calm down and come to terms with the situation, you may be able to start working together to solve it.

If you have reason to believe that your parents can't handle bad news and will abuse you physically or throw you out of the house, ask another adult to be present when you tell them. It might be a relative, friend, or clergyman whom you all respect and trust.

If you can't think of anyone to turn to, call one of the family counseling or social service agencies that are listed in the Yellow Pages. Family Service and Catholic Charities are two of the best known.

12. Somebody Else's Good News

It's impossible not to be jealous when your best friend makes the soccer team, falls in love, or gets straight A's— and you don't. It can drive you even crazier when it happens to someone you don't particularly like. Instead of sulking or making sour-grapes remarks, try not to show how rotten you feel.

It would be hypocritical to say you're happy about a friend's good news—and you'd need the acting talents of an Oscar winner to make him believe you. You'll find it easier to get the words out and be more convincing, too, if you address yourself to the other person's feelings; for example, "You must feel terrific," or "You must be so excited," or "This is really your lucky day."

Don't wait. Silence can be another form of hostility. Say something as soon as you hear the news.

You'll encounter all sorts of disappointments in life, and every one of them will hurt. But it isn't fair to let your bad feelings dampen somebody else's pleasure. Or to complicate your disappointment with the knowledge that you're being a sorehead, too.

Learn to act like a good loser even when you don't feel like one. Things will go your way another time. When they do, be a good winner, and tread lightly on the feelings of the people who weren't so lucky. You, of all people, should know how they feel.

If you've read this book carefully, you know how to cope with most of the situations that leave people speechless. You're sure to encounter others that will take you by surprise. Here's one last piece of advice to fall back on when you do: if you can't think of what to say, come right out and say so—"I'm so nervous (angry, upset, stunned, sorry, confused, delighted, or whatever) that I don't know what to say."

That may be enough. In any case, letting your secret out of the bag will make it seem less terrible. Your tensions will subside, your tongue will come untied, and you may very well think of the perfect thing to say.

Index